FORGING OUR LEGACY

Canadian Citizenship and Immigration, 1900–1977

VALERIE KNOWLES

AUTHOR'S ACKNOWLEDGEMENTS

The author wishes to acknowledge the invaluable help of Judith Turnbull, who did a preliminary editing of the manuscript, and Dr. Bruce Nesbitt of Jordan, Nesbitt and Associates Ltd., who completed the job and piloted the work through to completion. Thanks are also due to Brian Coleman for carefully checking facts and supplying some key information.

— V.K.

PUBLISHER'S ACKNOWLEDGEMENTS

As part of our activities celebrating the fiftieth anniversary of the *Canadian Citizenship Act* (1947), Citizenship and Immigration Canada commissioned this book by Valerie Knowles. The department is grateful to her, and to our sponsors for their encouragement and support:

Air Canada
BC TEL
Bell Canada
Bombardier Inc.
Canadian Airlines
Canadian Bankers Association
Canadian National
Mitel Corporation
Molson Breweries
NOVA Corporation
Petro-Canada
Power Corporation of Canada
Rogers Communications Inc.

Many members of the department helped in seeing the volume into print, and we thank them all: notably the editorial board comprising Rosaline Frith, Agnès Jaouich, Gerry Maffre, Gilles Pelletier, Claire Pilon, Donald Pineau, Danielle Racette, and Georges Tsaï; and the production team of Margo Nielsen, Thea Vandenberg, and Debbie Farnand. Translation services were deftly supplied by the Translation Bureau, an agency of Public Works and Government Services Canada. Proofreading was performed by Robert Drysdale

The opinions expressed in this book are those of the author, and do not necessarily reflect federal government policy or opinion.

Table of Contents

Preface

To commemorate the fiftieth anniversary of the *Canadian Citizenship Act* (1947), Citizenship and Immigration Canada, in conjunction with private-sector partners, commissioned this book. A survey history, it traces the evolution of Canadian citizenship and the role played by immigration in the development of Canada from the turn of the century until 1977, when the last major amendment to the *Citizenship Act* was made.

Canadian citizenship as we know it today was only ushered into existence in 1947, when the *Canadian Citizenship Act* came into force. That January, in an historic ceremony in a crowded Supreme Court chamber, 26 proud individuals received citizenship certificates under the new Act, which had been inspired by a visit made to war graves in France by Paul Martin Sr., then Secretary of State. As befits an occasion marking a prominent milestone in Canada's constitutional development, there was both glittering pageantry and moving moments. Fifty years later, in the same location, pageantry and stirring moments would figure prominently in still another citizenship ceremony commemorating important milestones in Canada's nationhood.

In the years leading up to 1947 and beyond, Canada's identity has been developed and shaped, in large part, by the contributions made by successive waves of immigrants. These waves are described in this book, which also shows how immigration, along with other key events in the country's development, contributed to the growth of Canadian nationalism and Canada's sense of identity, both of which culminated in the *Canadian Citizenship Act* of 1947 and the *Citizenship Act* of 1977.

CHAPTER 1

Introduction

Immigration, the entrance of people into a country for the purpose of settling there, has always played a central role in Canada's history. It was as much a feature of ancient times, when the ancestors of Canada's native peoples migrated from Asia by land via Beringia or by sea via the Japanese current,[1] as it is of the present day, when immigrants from around the world come to this country in the thousands.

At no time has immigration played a greater role in Canadian history than during the twentieth century. In fact, without the immigrants who have settled in all areas of the country since the turn of the century, Canada would not be the culturally rich, prosperous, and progressive nation that it is today. The flood of people that poured into Canada between 1900 and 1914 and the dramatic changes in immigration patterns that occurred in more recent decades created a present-day population that bears little resemblance to the population in 1900.

A snapshot of Canada in 1900 reveals a country with only seven provinces (Prince Edward Island, Nova Scotia, New Brunswick, Quebec, Ontario, Manitoba, and British Columbia) and a population of only 5,371,315, most of which is strung out along a narrow corridor just north of the American border. In this population, Aboriginal peoples number approximately 127,000 (2.4 percent), while people of British origin account for the largest part, numbering 3,063,195 (57 percent). Canadians of French origin, some 1,649,371 in number (30.7 percent), are concentrated in Quebec, which was settled by the French between 1608 and 1759. Small and relatively insignificant numbers of people of Scandinavian and central, southern, and east European origin have made their homes in Montréal, Toronto, Winnipeg, Edmonton, and across the Prairies.

In this turn-of-the-century snapshot, small pockets of Canadians of Asiatic origin can be found scattered

Chinese immigrant railway worker in British Columbia, circa 1922.

British Columbia Archives and Records Service (HP 69844)

---

[1] Canada's Aboriginal peoples commonly believe that they have lived on Canadian soil from the beginning of time and that various myths of theirs support this position.

across the country, although their numbers are concentrated in British Columbia. Especially noteworthy are survivors from among the 15,000 Chinese who were brought to Canada between 1880 and 1885 to toil on the British Columbia leg of the Canadian Pacific Railway. When work on the main railway line was finished in 1885, thousands of these Chinese were forced to migrate across the country in search of work.

Fast-forward to 1971 and the last Canadian census of ethnic origin conducted within the time frame of this book. Now we find a significantly different picture. We discover that Canada boasts a population of 21,568,310. In this population, Aboriginal peoples number 312,760 (1.5 percent), while people of British origin number 9,624,115 (44.6 percent) and Canadians of French origin 6,180,120 (28.7 percent). There are 1,317,200 people of German origin (6.1 percent) and 730,820 Canadians of Italian origin (3.4 percent). Canadians of Ukrainian origin number 580,660 (2.7 percent), while Canadians of Asian origin number 285,540 (1.3 percent). By 1996, one in ten Canadians will be neither white nor Aboriginal and visible minorities will make up nearly one-third of Vancouver's population and a corresponding portion of Toronto's. It is to immigration that we owe these changes in Canada's ethnic composition since the turn of the century.

Ever since France began dispatching settlers in the early seventeenth century to its tiny fur-trading post on the St. Lawrence River, successive waves of immigrants have left their own distinctive mark on Canadian society. In the closing years of the eighteenth century, these included some 40,000 to 50,000 Loyalists, refugees from the newly established United States of America who settled in what is now southern Quebec, Ontario, and the Maritime provinces. The first half of the nineteenth century saw a huge influx of British immigrants transform the face of Ontario. And, as noted, this century has seen the greatest changes, whether as a result of the Asian, South American, and Caribbean influxes of recent decades or of the streams of immigrants from continental Europe, Great Britain, and the United States in

Canadian census of ethnic origin, 1971

We discover that Canada boasts a population of 21,568,310.

Aboriginal origin	312,760	1.5%
British origin	9,624,115	44.6%
French origin	6,180,120	28.7%
German origin	1,317,200	6.1%
Italian origin	730,820	3.4%
Ukrainian origin	580,660	2.7%
Asian origin	285,540	1.3%

the opening years of the century, each group bringing the labour, capital, skills, and cultural diversity that are so essential to the building of a new country.

Continental Europeans did not settle in Canada in significant numbers in the early years of Confederation, but by the time that the fledgling dominion was sending soldiers to South Africa to fight in the Boer War (1899–1902), they had begun to arrive in unprecedented numbers. Of the almost 3 million immigrants who made their way to Canada between 1900 and the outbreak of the First World War in 1914, more than 500,000 came from continental Europe. This was Canada's first great wave of European immigration. Also, during these years, close to a million people emigrated from the British Isles, which continued to furnish Canada with its largest number of immigrants, and more than 750,000 arrived from the United States, many of them returning Canadians.

This huge influx of people represented a watershed in Canadian immigration history. From that time until

Thanks to these waves of humanity settling in our country, Canada has developed a much more cosmopolitan outlook and a much richer and more vibrant culture. This is especially true of the last few decades, which have seen striking new industrial and technological initiatives, a new burgeoning of the arts, and the development of a keen interest in and appreciation of the cuisine of faraway countries.

today, Canada has never received the number of immigrants that it did in 1913, when over 400,000 newcomers arrived on Canadian soil. But throughout this century immigrants did continue to choose Canada as their new country, and a second great wave (the last one to date) occurred between 1947 and 1961. Although this wave, like the first, featured newcomers from continental Europe, southern Europe, especially Italy, and central Europe became much more important sources of immigrants. By contrast, immigration from Great Britain declined substantially from the earlier period (1900–1914).

Thanks to these waves of humanity settling in our country, Canada has developed a much more cosmopolitan outlook and a much richer and more vibrant culture. This is especially true of the last few decades, which have seen striking new industrial and technological initiatives, a new burgeoning of the

arts, and the development of a keen interest in and appreciation of the cuisine of faraway countries. Large numbers of immigrants in our present-day cities have also thrust the immigration question into the political spotlight and made the ethnic vote a significant factor in many communities.

Beyond shaping Canada's social, economic, and political culture, immigration has served an even more vital function, one that is inextricably linked to this country's low birth rate. Canada's annual rate of population growth (natural increase plus net migration) has declined steadily in recent decades, from 3 percent in the late 1950s to less than 1 percent in the late 1990s. Much of this decline can be ascribed to the steep plunge in fertility rates after the baby boom period, largely the result of more women entering or re-entering the work force. In 1959, the fertility rate was four children per woman, but

by 1998 the rate had dropped to less than two per woman, considerably below the replacement level. Should this low fertility rate continue—and all indications are that it will—immigration will become essential for this country's healthy growth and even, perhaps, for its survival. At the time of the 1996 census, 17.4 percent of the people living in Canada were first-generation immigrants, the highest proportion in 50 years.

Recognizing the critical role that immigration plays in its development, Canada has put into place an active program for selecting and settling newcomers who will become full Canadian citizens. Only a handful of other countries have such a program. Canada also distinguishes itself by accepting more immigrants and refugees for permanent settlement in proportion to its population than any other country in the world.

A Ukrainian's Story

In its broad outline, Senefta Kizyma's story is typical of the saga of many Ukrainians who settled in Canada in the years immediately preceding the First World War.

Senefta Kizyma, née Rybka, was born in 1898 in Bukovina (a province of the Austro-Hungarian Empire), the daughter of poor peasants, whose worldly possessions included a small house, a tiny plot of land, a cow, and a few domestic fowl. To support his wife and two surviving children, her father worked in Romania, Bessarabia, and Moldavia, and supplemented his income by repairing shoes.

Dreaming of a better life, her father made three trips to Canada. On the third voyage, in 1912, he brought his entire family with him. Not every member wanted to make the move. Before leaving her native village, Senefta's mother cried bitterly because the family was leaving their homeland and striking out for a strange faraway country.

The Rybkas travelled from Antwerp, Belgium to Montréal by cattle boat. From there, they set off by train for the West, intending to settle on a homestead near Edmonton. Their plans changed abruptly, however, when a railway section foreman, an acquaintance of her father, intercepted the family as they were about to change trains in Calgary and persuaded Mr. Rybka to stay in that frontier town. Abandoning his dream of homesteading, the family head undertook "various kinds of city work for a living."

Fourteen-year-old Senefta, who had only a grade five education, initially worked alongside her mother in a boarding house owned by the railway foreman. Later she obtained employment as a domestic in the home of a "wealthy" family, who paid her ten dollars a month. In 1915, she went to work as a dishwasher in a restaurant.

Regrettably, Canada's entry into the First World War served to intensify long-festering prejudices against European immigrants, particularly those who had come from countries with which Canada was then at war. As "enemy aliens," members of the Ukrainian-Canadian community faced a lot of hostility. Thousands of hapless Ukrainians were even interned. Senefta was not interned, but she did lose her job. She was dismissed after a party of drunken soldiers stormed into the restaurant where she worked and ordered the owner to fire all his "Austrian" employees (in those days Ukrainians were referred to as Austrians). Senefta's father also lost his job because he was an "Austrian."

Following his dismissal, the family head worked as a miner in the Canmore district of Alberta. There, a passing policeman spotted some imported German tobacco tins on the family window sill. Convinced that the tins represented a deliberate flaunting of sympathy with the German cause, he arranged to have Senefta's father arrested. Only his wife's pleading spared him from incarceration. Having escaped this fate, Mr. Rybka suffered a crushed foot in a mine accident. Maimed for life, and with no compensation, he returned to Calgary with his family. Once again Senefta went to work in a restaurant, this time as a waitress, and joined a newly formed union that called a strike in the city's hotels and restaurants.

In Calgary, Senefta Rybka met and married Gregory Kizyma, a Canmore coal miner. After their marriage in 1918, the couple settled in Canmore, where Mr. Kizyma was active in the coal miners' union and where both he and his wife worked for the local branch of the Ukrainian Labour Temple Association. When the Great Depression robbed him of his job, the couple returned to Calgary to live with her parents.

Senefta Kizyma became very active in the Ukrainian Labour–Farmer Temple Association, the Canadian Peace Congress, and the Voice of Women following her return to Calgary. When interviewed for a book published in 1991 (Peter Krawchuk, *Reminiscences of Courage and Hope*), she had been involved in the Ukrainian progressive movement for over 50 years and could recall vividly the circumstances surrounding her family's emigration to Canada almost 80 years ago.

CHAPTER 2

The Arrival of the Europeans

**Sir Clifford Sifton,
Minister of the Interior, 1896–1905.**

National Archives of Canada (PA 027943)

Canada's first great wave of European immigration

Canada's first great wave of European immigration followed a lacklustre period in its immigration history. Despite the best efforts of Sir John A. Macdonald's Conservative government to attract newcomers, large-scale immigration failed to become a reality in the first three decades after Confederation in 1867. Canada's immigration prospects only started to look up in the 1890s, when the economic depression (1873–96) that had gripped Europe and North America ended and demand soared for Canadian foodstuffs, particularly hard wheat.

Fortunately for Canada, the reinvigorated economy coincided with a population explosion in Europe and a rapidly dwindling supply of good free land in the United States. Then, too, there was the election of Sir Wilfrid Laurier's Liberal government in 1896, which immediately launched an aggressive campaign to encourage settlement of the West.

Clifford Sifton and his policies

The principal planner and promoter of the campaign for western settlement was Clifford Sifton, who at the age of 35 was appointed Minister of the Interior in Laurier's new government. In this powerful portfolio, the six-foot dynamo exploited his renowned drive and relentless energy to the full and in so doing became the most celebrated and remarkable figure in Canadian immigration history.

Born in Ontario in 1861, Sifton moved with his family to Manitoba in 1875. He studied at Victoria College in Toronto and then returned to Manitoba to practise law in Brandon with his brother Arthur. Using law as a springboard, he embarked on a 23-year political career, beginning in the provincial arena, where he became a member of the Manitoba legislature and then an influential member of the Greenway Liberal government from 1891 to 1896. After presiding over the affairs of the Attorney General's Department and matters relating to education and provincial Crown lands, he accepted Laurier's invitation to become federal Minister of the Interior. Sifton spent his

This Norwegian poster is typical of the posters employed in Canada's aggressive campaign to attract European settlers to the West. Issued in the 1890s, it reads "Canada: 160 acres of free land for every settler."

issue of separate schools in the newly created provinces of Saskatchewan and Alberta.

A man of strong views as well as a born organizer, Sifton was determined to develop a well-organized Immigration Branch within his ministry and to fill the empty Prairies with suitable farmers as rapidly as possible. Having always been a provincial booster, the new Minister had unbounded confidence in the West. Furthermore, he was firmly convinced that massive agricultural immigration was the key to Canadian prosperity; it was his view that if primary resources were developed through the labour of hard-working immigrants, then industry and commerce would follow in their wake without the need of similar infusions of newcomers.

As soon as he arrived in Ottawa, Sifton set about making the Department of the Interior's Immigration Branch more efficient. He then simplified the

regulations of the *Dominion Lands Act,* the 1872 piece of legislation that granted a quarter section of free land (160 acres or 64.7 hectares) to any settler 21 years of age or older who paid a ten-dollar registration fee, lived on his quarter section for three years, cultivated 30 acres (12.1 hectares), and built a permanent dwelling. By ruthlessly pruning the Act's red tape, Sifton enabled immigrants to secure their promised homesteads more quickly.

Next came an assault on the lands that the federal government had granted to the railways in the 1880s to help them defray the costs of construction and to serve as collateral for railway bonds. Large blocks of these lands in the Prairie West had remained closed to free homesteading because the railways had selected only a small portion of them for sale to companies and individuals. It was a situation that clamoured for attention and Sifton met the

entire federal career in this portfolio, resigning in 1905 after a bitter disagreement with the Prime Minister over the

Dominion Lands Act, the 1872 piece of legislation that granted a quarter section of free land (160 acres or 64.7 hectares) to any settler 21 years of age or older who paid a ten-dollar registration fee, lived on his quarter section for three years, cultivated 30 acres (12.1 hectares), and built a permanent dwelling.

challenge by abolishing the land grants system and pressuring the railways, chiefly the Canadian Pacific Railway (CPR), into freeing land for general settlement.

Selling the West

Just as important as his political and organizational talents were Clifford Sifton's skills as a salesman, and these he applied aggressively to his far-reaching program to attract farmers and farm labourers to the West. While he employed methods that were not always new, he pursued these more vigorously than had been done previously in advertising the West's attractions. A torrent of pamphlets in several languages flooded Great Britain, Europe, and the United States. Canadian exhibits were mounted at fairs, exhibitions, and public displays, while "editorial articles," commissioned by his department, were inserted in foreign newspapers. Foreign journalists were wined and dined on guided tours across the West, and prosperous homesteaders were encouraged to revisit their homelands and those friends and relatives they had left behind, since it was Sifton's belief that the most effective advertising was done by individual contact.

Courting Americans

As a staunch member of the British Empire, Canada had hitherto sought British immigrants and it continued to do so during the Sifton years. In his quest for suitable agriculturalists to farm the West, however, Clifford Sifton stressed new fields for recruiting immigrants. One of these was the United States. Sir John A. Macdonald's government had generally regarded the U.S. as a competitor for new immigrants, but the Minister saw Canada's southern neighbour as itself a vast reservoir of potential new settlers. Instead of concentrating on the repatriation of former Canadians living south of the border, which had been the Conservatives' approach, the Department of the Interior under Sifton's direction expanded its network of American offices and agents and mounted a strong campaign to attract experienced American farmers with capital. Estimates indicate that between 1901 and 1914, over 750,000 immigrants entered Canada from the United States. While many were returning

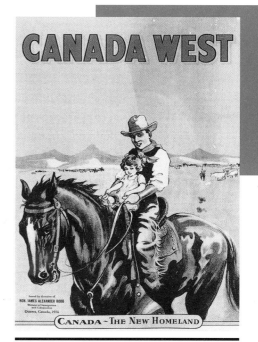

This poster was reproduced in the magazine *Canada West*, circa 1900–1920.

National Archives of Canada (C 30623)

Canadians, about one-third were new-comers of European extraction—Germans, Hungarians, Norwegians, Swedes, and Icelanders—who had originally settled in the American West.

As it had been in the past, the primary attraction for these American immigrants was good land, which was available in abundance on the Prairies and at no cost if the settlers met the conditions stipulated by Canada's homestead policy. Because they were familiar with the demanding way of life in North America and many of them were also experienced prairie farmers, most of these American homesteaders adapted well to conditions on the Prairies. Those who came with capital, machinery, and livestock—and many did—successfully settled into life in their new surroundings even more quickly. For this reason, Americans were considered to be among the most desirable of immigrants.

Sifton's campaign to attract American farmers was so effective that Americans constituted the largest group of immigrant settlers in the provinces of Saskatchewan and Alberta when they were created in 1905. The enthusiasm with which most Canadians greeted these American newcomers was summed up in the Lethbridge *Herald* in 1905:

> *Less enthusiastic were those Canadians who worried that these American settlers, because of their sheer numbers, would dominate development in the West, seizing control of its industry and edging the Prairies away from Britain and Canada and into the American sphere of influence. This concern was not shared, however, by the federal government, which continued to seek settlers from the United States during this period.*

No welcome mat for black Americans

When it came to prospective American settlers, the Immigration Branch solicited only white farmers, especially those living on the prairies and in the Midwest states. No attempt was made to recruit black agriculturalists, for they were widely regarded as being cursed with the burden of their African ancestry.

As unwelcome as black settlers were, no law was passed to exclude them, although administrators devised careful procedures to ensure that most applications submitted by black people were rejected. Private schemes for black settlement were also discouraged. For the most part, however, American black people expressed no great interest in coming to this country; they were too impoverished to contemplate emigration.

In its attempts to exclude black settlers, the Immigration Branch undoubtedly reflected public opinion in the West and elsewhere in Canada. Thousands of free black people had been among the Loyalists who had settled in Nova Scotia

Between 1901 and 1914, over 750,000 immigrants entered Canada from the United States. While many were returning Canadians, about one-third were newcomers of European extraction—Germans, Hungarians, Norwegians, Swedes, and Icelanders—who had originally settled in the American West.

in 1783. Later, runaway slaves from the United States had obtained refuge in Canada. Nevertheless, white settlers insisted that the Prairies be kept white, and in 1910, when it appeared that their wishes might be disregarded, they drove home this point. On learning that anti-black sentiment in the newly created state of Oklahoma threatened to drive a large migration of black Americans north to the Edmonton area, the citizens of Alberta's capital mounted a strong protest against Negro immigration. This spurred the Edmonton Municipal Council to pass a resolution urging the federal government to "take all action necessary to prevent the expected influx of Negroes" and the city's Board of Trade to petition the federal government to act immediately to prevent any black people from immigrating into Western Canada.

The anti-black backlash in Western Canada played directly into the hands of Immigration Branch officials who wanted to see the Canadian border closed to black immigration. Legislative action, they insisted, was the only answer. Accordingly, in 1911 these officials took unprecedented steps to have Canada acquire an exclusion ordinance

A group of immigrant women in front of the YMCA boarding house at 698 Ontario Street, Toronto, 1917.

National Archives of Canada (PA 126710)

against black settlers. Their efforts came to nought, however, because a general election that September threw the Liberals out of office before the necessary Order in Council could be drawn up and implemented. Years later, immigration authorities would resort to other methods to keep black settlers out of this country.

Immigrants in sheepskin coats: the Ukrainians

Clifford Sifton's second new field of recruitment was eastern and central Europe. In his urgent search for suitable farmers and farm labourers, the new Minister was prepared to admit agriculturalists from places other than Great Britain, the United States, and northern Europe, long the preferred suppliers of immigrants for Canada. Describing what he looked for in the ideal settler, Sifton said:

When I speak of quality I have in mind something that is quite different from what is in the mind of the average writer or speaker upon the question of immigration. I think that a stalwart peasant in a sheepskin coat, born on the soil, whose forefathers have been farmers for ten generations, with a stout wife and a half-dozen children, is good quality.

———————————

Clifford Sifton was quite correct when he noted that his view of the ideal settler to pioneer the West differed substantially from that held by most others who concerned themselves with the issue. The vast majority of English-speaking Canadians deplored the idea of Canada's admitting "illiterate Slavs in overwhelming numbers." Nevertheless, by dint of his forceful personality, status, and determination, Sifton managed to proceed with his controversial plan.

Unusual measures had to be put in place to attract "stalwart peasants" who would push back the western frontier and furnish seasonal or casual labour when required. One of these saw Sifton's department enter into a secret arrangement with a clandestine organization of booking agents and steamship company officials based in Amsterdam. According to the terms of the arrangement, known as the North Atlantic Trading Company contract, the North Atlantic Trading Company agreed to direct, whenever possible, agriculturalists to Canada; for its part, the Immigration Branch would give the company a bonus for every genuine agricultural settler steered to this country. The syndicate's operations and its members' names were kept secret because most European countries had restrictive emigration laws; in some, agents involved in immigration propaganda were liable to prosecution.

The government did everything it could to establish bloc settlements of the different ethnic groups and in this way attract immigration of the right kind. Such settlements, it was believed, would exert a powerful magnetic effect, and often they did. The Ukrainians (the collective name applied to Slavs from regions of the Russian and Austro-Hungarian empires in eastern and southern Europe) were by far the largest group to immigrate to Canada from eastern and central Europe in these years. Between 1891, when the first wave of Ukrainian immigrants came to Canada, and the outbreak of the First World War, approximately 170,000 Ukrainians settled in this country, attracted by the offer of free land, a sense of space, and an opportunity to make a living in a free and open society.

For the most part, these Ukrainian newcomers were small farmers and labourers from Galicia and Bukovina (both provinces of the Austro-Hungarian Empire) who were fleeing oppressive social and economic conditions in their homeland. Commonly called Galicians, because Galicia had furnished the first Ukrainians to immigrate to Canada, they headed for those parts of the West that provided meadow, water, wood, and, if possible, contact with pioneers who spoke their language. As a result, large numbers of Ukrainians settled in the aspen parkland of the Prairie provinces, a wide band of country that runs in an arc from southeastern Manitoba through central Saskatchewan to the Rocky Mountain foothills west of Edmonton. Today the route that these newcomers took is known as the Yellowhead Highway or Highway 16, also referred to as the Ukrainian Settlement Road.

When they first settled on the Canadian prairie, the Ukrainians continued to practise their traditional mixed farming, and their early settlements were distinguished by whitewashed huts with thatched roofs similar to those they had left behind. As they became better educated and more prosperous, they adopted frame houses, modern machinery, and advanced agricultural techniques. While pioneering huge tracts of land, the Ukrainians struggled to maintain and develop their language and culture. To this end, they founded the Prosvita (Enlightenment) Society. The Manitoba government aided their cause by establishing a training school in 1905 for Ukrainian teachers in Winnipeg. Further progress would be made after the Second World War, when several Canadian universities, along with a number of other Canadian institutions of higher learning, established Ukrainian language and literature programs and the provinces of Saskatchewan, Alberta, and Manitoba introduced optional credit courses in Ukrainian at the high school level.

German immigrants arriving in Québec City, 1911.

National Archives of Canada (PA 10254)

The Ukrainian community, through its dedication to its traditions, has made many cultural contributions to Canadian life, some of them dating from the first decades of this century. These have included a Ukrainian travelling theatre, which appeared in the West as early as 1915, and a school of Ukrainian folk dancing, which was established in 1926.

German immigration

Among the thousands of immigrants who homesteaded on the Prairies in these years were settlers of German origin. Most came not from the German Empire, but from the Russian and the Austro-Hungarian empires and the Balkan countries, where German colonies had been established in the eighteenth century. By the closing decades of the nineteenth century, several factors affecting these settlements encouraged emigration. One was a shortage of land, the result of the colonies' rapid growth and the large size of many German-speaking families. The growing class of landless workers and a dearth of factory jobs also spurred the exodus. A further factor was nationalist sentiment that in some areas led to the repeal of the Germans' original rights and privileges.

From the 1890s until the outbreak of the First World War, approximately 35,000 Germans settled in Manitoba, representing 7.5 percent of that province's total population. Alberta (where Germans concentrated in the Medicine Hat area and along the Calgary and Edmonton Railway) and Saskatchewan also witnessed a dramatic growth in German immigration, in Saskatchewan's case from less than 5,000 in 1901 to over 100,000 in 1911. Most settlements in Saskatchewan broke down along denominational lines: Mennonites, the first to pioneer on the Prairies, settled in Swift Current and Rosthern; Lutherans, in central Saskatchewan; and Roman Catholics, after 1903, in St. Peter's Colony, near Humboldt, and in St. Joseph's Colony, near Trampling Lake.

Repatriation of French Canadians

The Canadian government welcomed French-speaking immigrants from France, but this country had a dismal record as a source of immigrants. France felt strongly that it needed its population, in particular a strong army to protect itself against German expansionism. As a result, the French government was generally opposed to emigration. When French citizens expressed an interest in leaving, they were encouraged to emigrate to French colonies. Accordingly, Ottawa concentrated on repatriating French Canadians who had been lured to New England by the prospect of good-paying factory jobs and the spell of American prosperity. To entice these Franco-Americans back to Quebec, the government employed French-Canadian priests and lay agents. Priests based in Quebec parishes received a small stipend to spend time in the United States promoting the idea of repatriation among Franco-Americans. To further the cause, the government also gave grants to colonization societies located in Montréal and Québec City.

Italian immigration

Canada did not actively seek Italian immigrants in this period because Clifford Sifton considered Italians ill-fitted for pioneering, placing them in the same category as artisans, clerks, common labourers, and other city

> **The Canadian government welcomed French-speaking immigrants from France, but this country had a dismal record as a source of immigrants. France felt strongly that it needed its population, in particular a strong army to protect itself against German expansionism. As a result, the French government was generally opposed to emigration.**

Giovanni Veltri's Story

Giovanni Veltri's story is typical of that of so many Italian men who left their southern Italian homeland at the turn of the century in search of work and entrepreneurial opportunity overseas.

Born into a peasant family in 1867, Veltri grew up in Grimaldi, a small town located high in the hills south of Cosenza in Italy's depressed south. Because his town had little to offer him, Veltri, with two cousins and a friend, set off in the early 1880s for northern Africa in search of work. There, he found employment helping to build a railway line between Batna and Biskra in Algeria. The teenager spent 16 months in this part of the world before leaving in 1885 to join a brother in the American northwest.

After enduring a 31-day sea voyage, Veltri arrived in the United States, where the gates had been recently opened to immigrants from eastern and southern Europe. He managed to find his older brother in Helena, Montana. Vincenzo had worked his way up to the position of foreman for one of the subcontractors hired by the Montana Central Railroad. Like his brother had before him, Giovanni Veltri went to work as a navvy (an unskilled labourer).

The two brothers spent almost two decades toiling in railway construction in both the American and Canadian northwest before deciding to stay in Canada. By this time, 1898, Canada's economic prospects were on the upswing and there was an air of buoyant optimism everywhere. The semi-arid prairie lands were being successfully farmed as a result of breakthroughs in agricultural technology, and immigrants had begun to pour into the West. All the conditions were ripe for an orgy of railway building.

The Veltri brothers were well poised to profit from the feverish railway building. Now seasoned railway workers, they exploited their expertise by successfully competing for subcontracts and by hiring gangs of labourers made up largely of Italians, often fellow Grimaldesi. To maximize their opportunities, the always pragmatic brothers anglicized their names. Veltri was replaced by Welch, Giovanni by John, and Vincenzo by James V.

By now Giovanni was a married man and a father. On one of his periodic visits to Grimaldi he had married Rosa Anselmo, who for many years stayed behind in Italy, there giving birth to Raffaele, "his first and dearest son." The marriage would produce five children. In 1905, Giovanni brought young Raffaele to Winnipeg, where he and Vincenzo had earlier established the family railway contracting business.

When Vincenzo, a bachelor, died in 1913, Giovanni Veltri inherited the family firm, which he renamed the John Welch Company. This was the name the firm would be known by for almost 20 years as it competed for railway subcontracts and hired work gangs composed principally of Italian labourers.

Giovanni Veltri finally brought his family over to Canada in 1924, settling them first in Winnipeg and then in Port Arthur, Ontario (which amalgamated with the city of Fort William to form Thunder Bay in 1970). There, they made their home until late in 1931. In that memorable year, Giovanni, his wife, and unmarried daughters left Canada and returned to Grimaldi, where Giovanni cultivated his passion for agriculture and reverted to his Italian name, Giovanni Veltri.

Raffaele Veltri, upset by his parents' decision to leave Canada, remained in Port Arthur to head up the family company, which changed its name to R.F. Welch Ltd. Under his able guidance, the firm survived the Great Depression and the Second World War by undertaking maintenance work for Canadian National Railways. R.F. Welch's most lucrative contract was signed in the early 1950s when the company hired labourers destined for CNR work gangs and provided catering and commissary services for them.

Such was the achievement of the Veltri family that the Grimaldesi of Thunder Bay honoured Raffaele at a testimonial function in 1971. By that time there was a generous sprinkling of Italian names in the Thunder Bay city directory and Italy ranked second only to Great Britain as a source of immigrants for Canada.

Born in adjacent towns in Le Marche, a region of central Italy, Ilde Tontini and Ettore Saudelli immigrated to Canada in 1923 and 1912 respectively. The couple met in Montreal and married in 1928.

Leanna Verrucci Collection.

railways began in earnest, there was a further dramatic increase in the numbers of Italians coming to Canada.

Most of the Italians who came to this country between the turn of the century and the First World War, either from Italy or from the American east coast, were migrant workers, often bachelors. After working for the summer, many returned home to contribute their savings towards the upkeep of their southern Italian villages and the purchase of dowries for sisters and daughters. Those who did not make it back to Italy wintered in the railhead cities, notably Montréal.

When railway work was succeeded by labouring jobs for interurban and street railways, more Italians decided to stay in the cities. Instead of returning to Italy, young men chose to become immigrants and they sent for their wives or other relatives, thereby initiating a process of "chain-migration." In major Canadian cities, Italian business districts grew up and the ambience of Little Italy emerged; the padrone who had recruited unskilled labour for the railway companies was now joined by middle-class shopkeepers, importers,

dwellers. Thousands of Italians nevertheless came to Canada from Italy and from the "Little Italys" of the American east coast in these years. Most were peasants or sharecroppers, small landowners, and rural day labourers from the impoverished southern regions of Italy, where they had wrested a living from a harsh environment and struggled against an exploitative socioeconomic order. Confronting a bleak future in their homeland, these southern

Italians emigrated overseas in search of work and entrepreneurial opportunity.

From among those who arrived in Canada, thousands went to work for this country's railways. Others found employment in the mining and resource industries, where there was a demand for intensive labour. Some 3,000 Italians arrived in Montréal in 1904, and two years later, when construction of the trunk lines of the Grand Trunk Pacific, the Canadian Northern, and the National Transcontinental caterers, priests, and undertakers. By the time the First World War broke out, half of the fruit merchants in Toronto were of Italian descent.

Russian immigration

The first great wave of European immigration to Canada included the first Russians to settle in the country. They were Doukhobors, members of a peasant sect whose pacifism and communal lifestyle had invited czarist authorities to mount a campaign of brutal persecution and harassment against them. Fortunately for the Doukhobors, their plight aroused the sympathy of Leo Tolstoy, the great Russian novelist, who used his fame, literary skills, and international connections to help them to emigrate. A prominent Russian anarchist, Peter Kropotkin, and James Mavor of the University of Toronto also aided their cause, the latter persuading the Canadian authorities to admit sect members to Canada. In late January 1899, the first of five parties of Doukhobors, numbering over 7,500 people, settled in the Prince Albert and

Yorkton areas in what is now the province of Saskatchewan.

Although the Doukhobors were permitted to establish community settlements, each settler was required to make his own entry for a homestead and to take an oath of allegiance within three years in order to obtain title to his property. The Doukhobors, however, refused to have any dealings with the state. They refused to take the oath, and they would not register births, marriages, and deaths; neither would they allow their children to be educated in the public system. As the three-year probationary period drew to a close, splits appeared in the community. These were widened by the actions of an extremist group, the Sons of Freedom, who liberated cattle, burnt property, and refused to till the land. At the other end of the scale were a number of Doukhobors who broke away from the community, took the oath of allegiance, and began to farm their land and to live

and work like other settlers. In between were the rest of the Doukhobors, who attempted to maintain the traditional community pattern while being harassed by the Sons of Freedom.

Order was finally restored by the Doukhobors' spiritual leader Peter Veregin. After arriving in the Northwest Territories in 1903, he quickly set about reorganizing the sect members into a prosperous farming community and keeping the Sons of Freedom under control. In 1908, Veregin purchased a large tract of land in British Columbia (the oath of allegiance was not a requirement in that province), organized the Doukhobors as the Christian Community of Universal Brotherhood, and established community villages in the province. Here, too, independent-minded members broke away to take their place in the outside society.

Apart from the Doukhobors, very few Russians entered Canada before the First World War. Canada was not a

Apart from the Doukhobors, very few Russians entered Canada before the First World War. Canada was not a popular destination for emigrating Russians; for them, western Europe, the United States, and South America were the favoured destinations.

popular destination for emigrating Russians; for them, western Europe, the United States, and South America were the favoured destinations. Nevertheless, small Russian communities developed in Sydney, Montréal, Toronto, Windsor, Timmins, Winnipeg, Vancouver, and Victoria. Most of the Russians in these communities had been peasant farmers who had left their homeland because of their intense opposition to the czarist regime. After arriving in this country, many found jobs in Canada's growing industrial sector.

British immigration

Although there were relatively few good agriculturalists left to court in the "mother country," the Canadian government continued to promote immigration from the United Kingdom—often called Great Britain or simply Britain—during the Sifton years, principally because English Canadians took it for granted that their federal government would do everything possible to retain the British character of the country. Prior to 1903, Canada's immigration service in Britain had been under the control of the Canadian High Commission, but in January of that year immigration was removed from its jurisdiction. To handle immigration, Sifton established an emigration office in London that would be effectively independent of the high commissioner's office.

The new office was housed in Trafalgar House, an imposing building that commanded a central location overlooking the historic open space of Trafalgar Square. As one enthusiastic observer remarked:

No one passing to and from the Houses of Parliament and official Westminster can fail to notice "Trafalgar House." The eye is caught at once by the familiar Canadian "Arch" of Coronation days, a representation of which is emblazoned on one of the windows, whilst elsewhere the intending emigrant is invited to enter by the mottoes, "Improved Farms at Reasonable Prices," "Healthy Climate, Light Taxes, Free Schools," "160-acre Free Farms."

———————

The establishment of an independent emigration office in a central location in London paved the way for a dramatic increase in British immigration. In the first six months of 1900, just over 5,000 Britons came to Canada. Five years later the annual number soared to above 65,000, exceeding the numbers of new settlers arriving from the United States.

Most British newcomers in this pre-war period emigrated to Canada in hopes of finding a higher standard of living and freedom from the rigidities of the hallowed British class system. Included in the ranks of these unsponsored immigrants were not only people of modest means but also individuals with substantial funds who would often invest in large-scale ranching or farming ventures in Western Canada.

Many of these well-heeled middle- and upper-class Britons had set off for Canada because it was difficult to find suitable employment in Britain's amply supplied and highly competitive professions. Others had left large estates burdened by heavy debts and tithes. For these prosperous Britons, emigration seemed to offer the only way that they could maintain their own and their children's lifestyle in a rapidly changing world. They chose Canada largely because of the efforts of the emigration and booking agents, the aggressive campaigns mounted by Canadian colonization companies, and the seductive promotional material that extolled the attractions of the various provinces for "gentlemen emigrants."

Not all of these well-off British newcomers were warmly welcomed in their adopted country. In fact, there was widespread resentment against those of them who seemed to expect special treatment in the "colony." Not infrequently, employment ads in western newspapers included the words "No English need apply." And when the London reporter H.R. Whates was researching the immigration boom for an article for the London *Standard* in 1905, Canadians bluntly informed him: "The Englishman is too cocksure; he is too conceited, and he thinks he knows everything and he won't try to learn our ways."

The great influx from Britain in these years also included poor immigrants who had been assisted by charitable organizations wanting to rid the United Kingdom of paupers and help them make a fresh start in the colonies. One of the many philanthropic agencies involved in this endeavour was the Salvation Army, which was established in Canada in 1882. From 1884, when a branch of the Church Army—the Self-Help Emigration Society—began its work, until 1914, the "Army next to God" assisted 150,000 of Great Britain's deserving poor to emigrate to Canada. The Salvation Army's immigration program did not escape controversy, however. Organized labour was especially hostile, charging the dominion government with paying the agency bonuses for recruiting individuals who posed as "agriculturalists" but soon became industrial workers.

The home children

Most of the British poor who emigrated to Canada in this first European wave came in families, but an impressive number did not. Conspicuous in the latter's ranks were thousands of young boys and girls who arrived in this country unaccompanied by an adult family member. These children, once

Galician immigrants, Québec City, Quebec, 1911.

National Archives of Canada (PA 010263)

A group of boys from Barnardo homes in England shown after their arrival in Belleville, Ontario, circa 1922.

here, were apprenticed as agricultural labourers or, in the case of girls, sent to smaller towns or rural homes to work as domestic servants.

These were the "home children," slum youngsters plucked from philanthropic rescue homes and parish workhouse schools and dispatched to Canada (and to other British colonies) to meet the soaring demand for cheap labour on Canadian farms and household labour in family homes. Many of these youngsters, most of whom ranged in age between eight and ten, came from families of the urban poor who could not care for them properly. Other children, perhaps one-third their number, were orphans, while the balance were runaways or abandoned youngsters. At a time when few British emigrants were indentured in their overseas destinations, nearly all these child immigrants were apprenticed shortly after their arrival in Canada.

Although Canadian farms had received orphaned and destitute British children as early as the 1830s, it was not until 1868 that the home-children movement began in an organized way. In that year, Maria Susan Rye, the feminist daughter of a distinguished London solicitor, purchased an old jail on the outskirts of Niagara-on-the-Lake, Ontario, had it refurbished, and then made preparations to bring her first party of children to Canada. They arrived in October 1869 with the well-publicized blessings of both the Archbishop of Canterbury and *The Times of London.*

A few months later, Annie Macpherson, a Quaker working independently of Rye, brought another party of young children to Ontario. Soon, Louisa Birt of Liverpool (Macpherson's sister), Thomas Barnardo of London, Leonard Shaw of Manchester, and William Quarrier of Glasgow—to name but a few of the best-known child-savers—were launching their own child-emigration programs. Before long there was a proliferation of similar programs, some of the more notable being implemented by the National Children's Homes, Mr. Fegan's Homes of Southwark and Westminster, the Middlemore Homes in Birmingham, the Church of England Waifs and Strays Society, and Miss Stirling of Edinburgh. Because Canada was closer to Britain than was Australia or New Zealand, it became the favoured destination for these charges, especially during the Sifton years.

Underlying all these schemes was the activists' belief that emigration was an effective way to rescue impoverished British children from the poorest and most crowded districts of Britain's teeming cities. On Canadian farms, far from the temptations and polluted air of city life, their slum protégés would grow into healthy, industrious adults. Or so the thinking went.

Among the many names closely associated with this unique immigration program, the one most familiar to Canadians was undoubtedly that of Irish-born Thomas John Barnardo. Barnardo's vanity and thirst for prestige led him to use the title "Doctor," although he had never completed his medical studies.

Born into a Dublin family of modest means in 1845, Barnardo headed to London in 1866 to train as a

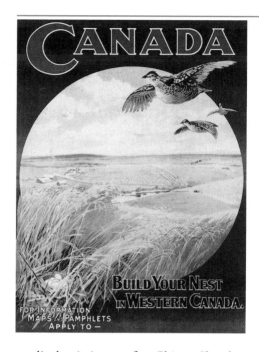

medical missionary for China. Shortly after his arrival in London, the young medical student came across the city's homeless waifs sleeping in its alleys and on its rooftops. The plight of London's homeless children so affected Barnardo that when he was rejected for missionary work in China, he abandoned all plans to be a physician and vowed to make helping these street children his life's work. To this end, the authoritarian trailblazer established a home for

boys in 1870, the first of his numerous homes for destitute children.

Initially Barnardo was able to find work for his protégés in Britain, but when employment opportunities started to dry up in both the trades and domestic service, he decided to explore emigration possibilities. In the autumn of 1882, he launched a comprehensive emigration program that would see some 30,000 children sent to Canada before it petered out in 1939.

Most of the Barnardo children led anonymous lives. One exception was George Everitt Green, a young agricultural labourer from England, although it would not be until after his death that Canadians would learn more about him than about any of the other home children dispatched to Canada. Only seven months after his arrival on an Ontario farm in 1895 Green was dead, his limbs gangrenous and his body emaciated and covered with sores, the visible marks of the cruel treatment dealt him by his spinster employer.

The inquest and trial that followed caused such a sensation that the federal and Ontario governments introduced legislation to prevent a similar tragedy from ever happening again. Even more far-reaching action was taken after three home children committed suicide in the winter of 1923–24. In the wake of these suicides, a British parliamentary delegation travelled to Canada to interview immigration officials, social workers, representatives of women's, labour, and farm organizations, and child immigrants themselves. Its findings led the delegation to declare that future child emigrants should be of working—

that is, school-leaving—age. Taking its cue from the delegation's report, Canada's Immigration Branch introduced a regulation in 1925 that prohibited voluntary immigration societies from bringing children under 14 years of age to this country. Intended to last three years, the ban was made permanent in 1928.

The long-lived program eventually came to a halt in 1939, its end hastened not only by the Great Depression and the opposition of the Canadian labour movement but also by a change of thinking on the part of Canadians and Britons. Both, it seems, could no longer tolerate the idea of philanthropic organizations separating young children from their parents and sending them to work in distant lands, no matter how salubrious the setting.

The Barr Colony

The Barr Colony does not appear on contemporary maps of Canada. Nevertheless, early in this century this British settlement on the plains of what became Saskatchewan attracted countless curious visitors and inspired many

column inches of print in daily newspapers in Canada and Britain.

The colony was noteworthy because it defied the belief held by many officials and journalists that a group of British immigrants without farming experience could survive on the bald prairie, 300 kilometres from the nearest city, without even a road or a rail line to link them to civilization. Within five years of the settlement's founding, these same sceptics were lauding the achievements of the Barr colonists. Their achievements were certainly remarkable but no more so than the journey that took them to the Canadian wilderness in the vicinity of present-day Lloydminster. This unforgettable migration was inspired by the lofty vision of two clerics, Isaac Barr (1847–1937), after whom the colony was named, and George Lloyd (1861–1940), who worked with the Colonial and Continental Church Society.

Canadian-born Isaac Barr was an Anglican clergyman who was fascinated by the career of Cecil Rhodes, the British diamond magnate and imperialist. He even attempted to join the famous Briton in a colonizing venture, leaving his Washington D.C. parish to travel to London in January 1902. But Rhodes died in March of that year, frustrating Barr's dream to serve the Empire by founding an overseas colony. Barr revived his plans, however, on learning of the Reverend George Lloyd's interest in organizing a settlement in Canada of unemployed British workers and soldiers demobilized from the Boer War. "Let us take possession of Canada," he wrote in a letter to *The Times of London* in 1902. "Let our cry be 'CANADA FOR THE BRITISH.'"

The two clerics joined forces to organize a Canadian settlement of almost 2,000 Britons, few of whom were of the sturdy farming stock traditionally considered necessary for successful homesteading. Barr handled nearly all the administrative arrangements. He persuaded the Canadian government to reserve a block of land for the settlers, collected settlers' fees, purchased supplies, and arranged for transportation. But he refused to act as a chaplain for the colonists, claiming that the colony was not to be an Anglican enclave in the prairie wilderness. As a result of this decision, the

In the 1880s, immigrants travelled by train to Western Canada.

Provincial Archives of Manitoba (N 7934)

Reverend George Lloyd and his family were persuaded to join the group at the last minute.

Unfortunately for the colonists, Barr was no altruist. Determined to reap financial gain from this venture, he received a commission from the Canadian government for each immigrant and worked in league with local merchants. He was also no organizing genius. Things began to go wrong the day that the *SS Lake Manitoba* sailed from the Old Country in 1903. After a rough ocean voyage in a ship equipped

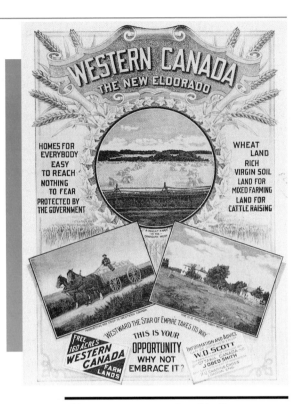

This poster was reproduced in the magazine *Canada West*, circa 1900–1914.

National Archives of Canada (C 85854)

to handle only about 550 passengers instead of 1,900, the exhausted immigrants arrived in Saint John, New Brunswick, where they faced countless delays and numerous baggage inspections. Eventually they boarded three

filthy immigrant trains, none of them with overnight accommodation, for the five-day trip to Saskatoon.

The settlers experienced further disillusionment when they arrived at Saskatoon. Army-surplus bell tents had been erected to house them, and since there was no station house, their luggage was dumped onto the prairie. Local merchants charged inflated prices for basic necessities, and Barr's promises of wagons, oxen, and other supplies were not kept. In addition to these hardships, the settlers then had to endure a long and arduous wagon journey along a primitive trail that for part of the way wound through sloughs and down steep cliffs before reaching North Battleford. For many of the colonists who had no experience driving oxen and wagons this challenge was too much and they turned back. The majority, however, persevered, stopping overnight in large marquee tents set up by immigration officials.

The remaining colonists' frustration with Barr finally boiled over in an explosive meeting in one of the trailside camps. Barr was accused of being in league with the Saskatoon merchants,

of failing to deliver on his promise of a transportation company and a co-operative store, and, worst of all, of misleading the colonists about conditions on the Prairies. Most of the people at the meeting voted to depose Barr as their leader, but they did not want to break up the colony. Instead, they renamed the venture "Britannia Colony" and voted in a new leadership, George Lloyd and an elected committee of twelve, soon dubbed the "Twelve Apostles."

After finally reaching the reserve in May 1903, the settlers and Lloyd began homesteading. Soon a village, named Lloydminster to honour the man who had gained the settlers' confidence, grew up along the fourth meridian. In their first year, many of the colonists came close to starving. They battled mosquitoes, blizzards, and prairie fires, but thanks to their hard work and perseverance the settlement survived and began to prosper. As early as 1905, three large hotels were under construction. The town's success was finally assured when the railway arrived in July of that year.

Barr, meanwhile, had returned to the United States, but not before being publicly pelted with rotten eggs by the people of Regina. After working in various secular jobs south of the border, he joined the Closer Settlement near Melbourne, Australia. The settlement failed, but Barr stayed on after the other settlers departed, never to move again.

Immigration to British Columbia

Not only the Prairies attracted a strong flow of immigrants in the early years of this century. British Columbia, which had entered Confederation in 1871, was also a magnet for newcomers. Admittedly, the volume of immigration to this province did not begin to approach that to the Prairies, but it was nevertheless impressive.

The British

Retired businessmen, farmers, and the younger sons in aristocratic families were among the British newcomers who flocked to Canada's most westerly province. Their attention was first drawn by advertising material describing

the joys of farming in lush interior valleys dotted with beautiful lakes filled with trout. Inspired further by the enthusiastic reports of Lord Aberdeen, Canada's Governor General from 1893 to 1898, well-to-do British immigrants purchased ranches and fruit farms in the Okanagan Valley, where the Scottish aristocrat had extensive properties.

The Japanese

Because British Columbia faced the Pacific Ocean, it drew many of its non-British newcomers from Asia, including Japan. Although the first known Japanese person to emigrate to Canada, Manzo Nagano, settled in the province in 1877, Japanese immigrants did not begin arriving in appreciable numbers until 1900. By 1914, however, only 10,000 Japanese had settled in the whole of Canada, by far the largest number in British Columbia.

The first wave of Japanese immigrants, called Issei, arrived between 1877 and 1928. Prior to 1907, most Japanese settlers were young men. In that year, at Canada's insistence, Japan limited the number of males who could emigrate to this country to 400 a year, thereby becoming the only nation to specifically control the movement of its people to Canada. As a consequence, for several years thereafter most of the immigrants from Japan were women who had come to join their husbands. In 1928, Canada and Japan revised the gentlemen's agreement of 1907 to restrict Japanese immigration to Canada to 150 persons annually, a quota that was rarely met. The Issei were invariably young and came from poor and overcrowded fishing and farming villages on the islands of Honshu and Kyushu.

Japanese coming ashore in Vancouver. The first gentleman was a member of a Japanese parliamentary delegation seeking amendment of British Columbia's oppressive policies towards immigration from Asia, 1899.

Selkirk College Library

Most settled in or near Vancouver and Victoria, in fishing villages and pulp towns along the Pacific coast, and on farms in the Fraser Valley.

The Sikhs

The first immigrants from India came to Vancouver and Victoria in 1904. Although British Columbia did its best to discourage non-white immigrants from Asia, barring them from the professions and denying them the right to vote, among other measures, some 5,000 immigrants from India had journeyed to the province by the end of 1907. Of these, the overwhelming majority were Sikhs (members of the reformist religion that originated about 1500 in the Punjab in northern India). The first Sikhs arrived in the province in 1904, having learned about its beauties and advantages from a detachment of Sikh soldiers who had returned home from London by way of Canada after attending Queen Victoria's Diamond Jubilee in 1897. Most of these early Sikh immigrants found work in the province's lumber mills and logging camps.

In 1999, a postage stamp was issued to commemorate the contributions that Sikh Canadians had made in the building of Canada. Among those present at the unveiling ceremony was Herb Dhaliwal, then the Minister of National Revenue, whose Sikh grandfather had come to Canada in 1906.

The Norwegians

In addition to Britons and Asiatics, Norwegians also settled in British Columbia in the early years of this century. Their ranks included a group that established a settlement at Grande Prairie in the Peace River District in 1908. Four years later another party of Norwegians founded the nearby settlement of Valhalla.

Non-agricultural settlement

Because Canada received substantial numbers of good agricultural settlers during its most intensive period of nation-building, it is safe to say that Clifford Sifton met one of his chief objectives. On the other hand, he failed miserably in his attempts to direct large numbers of immigrants away from the cities. Contrary to the popular perception of the young Canada, this was not a country that farmed and exploited primary resources alone; in fact, approximately 70 percent of the newcomers in this period obtained work in industry and transportation, where there was a soaring demand for their services.

At the very time that the last of the choicest land in the West was being brought under the plough, Canada was experiencing rapid industrial development. In one 20-year period, 1890–1910, the number of persons employed in manufacturing doubled; by the outbreak of the First World War, Canadians were earning as much from manufacturing as they were from agriculture. Such feverish activity in the manufacturing sector, coupled with a mad rush to build more transcontinental railways and open new mines, translated into a huge demand for labour.

For this reason, it is easy to see why so many immigrants were more tempted by the cities than by rural areas. Furthermore, it was not always easy for most of the new arrivals in Canada to take up farming right away. Then, as now, settling on the land was an expensive business, and newcomers, especially those from eastern, southern, and central Europe, rarely had the necessary funds to begin farming right away. As a result, many of them first obtained

Norwegian immigrants at Grand Trunk Railway Ferry in Québec City, circa 1911.

National Archives of Canada (PA 10394)

employment in manufacturing or transportation in Canada's cities and evolving industrial towns, while others found work in railway construction, lumbering, or mining. Even a good number of the immigrants who entered the agricultural force as wage labourers soon left this employment entirely to take up work elsewhere.

Opposition to immigration

Organized labour, of course, took a very jaundiced view of the hiring of unskilled immigrant labour by railways and manufacturing companies. One spokesman who did not hesitate to speak bluntly on the subject was James Wilks, a vice-president of the Trades and Labour Congress. In 1900, he wrote to Prime Minister Wilfrid Laurier about the impact that an influx of Scandinavians and Finns from Minnesota had on the Canadian labour market. Wilks beseeched the Laurier government to enforce the *Alien Labour Act,* a piece of legislation designed to prevent the importation of contract labour. Only rigorous enforcement of this law, claimed Wilks, would prevent Canada from being inundated with "ignorant, unfortunate…non-English-speaking aliens" who would do irreparable damage to the community.

There was also widespread opposition to western pioneers from central and southeastern Europe. Excellent farmers they might have been, but in the eyes of many westerners this did not qualify them as desirable settlers. Only those who assimilated readily into the dominant Anglo-Saxon society were welcome.

On the Prairies, suspicion and hatred of this kind were focussed mainly on the Ukrainians and the Doukhobors. In Winnipeg, the gateway to the West, the Ukrainians consistently equalled or outnumbered the combined totals of American and British arrivals between 1897 and 1899. It did not matter that less than half of the total number of immigrants to Canada in most years (and usually far less than half) were other than British in origin. What did matter was what was happening in Winnipeg. And from this vantage point, concerned westerners saw sizeable pockets of unassimilable ethnic groups sprouting across the West. The result was a heated debate about "Canadianization" and a cry for the government to be more selective about the types of immigrants that it let into the country. After Sifton left office in 1905, his successor, Frank Oliver, would heed this cry and chart a new course.

Cyril Genik:
"Czar of Canada"

Bizarre as it sounds, there was once a "Czar of Canada." He was not, of course, a real monarch, but a well-known and highly respected immigration officer. Cyril Genik, who lived from 1857 to 1925, was given his title by bewildered Ukrainian immigrants, happy to obey every command of a knowledgeable official who could help them in a new and strange land.

Like those he served, Cyril Genik was of Ukrainian origin. He came to this country in 1896, during the years of massive Ukrainian immigration to Canada (1896–1914). He headed the second group of Ukrainian immigrants dispatched to Canada during this period by Dr. Josef Oleskow, an agriculturalist who became known as "the father of organized Ukrainian immigration to Canada."

Most of Cyril Genik's compatriots were poorly educated peasants whose few worldly possessions had consisted of perhaps a small house, a tiny plot of land, a cow, and a few domestic fowl. Genik, by contrast, was a well-educated former teacher with a good knowledge of English and other languages.

Within a week of arriving in Winnipeg in July 1896, Genik and some of the men in his party left to reconnoitre agricultural land south of the city. By August, the settlers had chosen homesteads close to an established German Mennonite colony. The settlement that they founded, called Stuartburn, eventually became one of the largest Ukrainian colonies in Manitoba.

Although Genik registered his homestead, he and his family did not stay long in the new settlement. They soon returned to Winnipeg, where, in November 1896, Genik was hired by the federal government's Immigration Branch as a part-time interpreter. The volume of Ukrainian immigration increased so dramatically that in 1898 he became a full-time salaried worker. As such, he became the first Ukrainian to be employed as a full-time Canadian public servant.

Cyril Genik was described officially as an "interpreter," but his duties extended far beyond translation; he was expected to furnish many forms of guidance and assistance to Ukrainian immigrants as soon as possible after their arrival in Canada. Genik travelled to eastern ports to meet immigrant ships and then accompanied groups of Ukrainians on the train west. During the long train journey, he advised the newcomers on government homestead regulations, helped them to complete some of the preliminary arrangements, and held at bay swindling moneychangers and predatory merchants offering useless goods at exorbitant prices. Once the Ukrainians reached the prairies, Genik helped them choose land, register their homesteads, and find employment.

When they were settled, he visited their communities and reported to the federal government on their progress. In his Immigration Branch uniform, Cyril Genik became a familiar link between Canadian government officials and Ukrainian immigrants. As such, he played a valuable role in helping these newcomers adapt to the new and sometimes cruel land in which they had chosen to settle. And in easing the way for one group of immigrants, he emboldened other Ukrainians to leave home for Western Canada.

After his retirement in 1914, Cyril Genik continued to work as a leader in the Ukrainian–Canadian community, promoting various cultural causes, publishing articles, and, for a time, advocating the establishment of an independent Ukrainian church in Canada. His achievements were so many and so varied that by the time he died, Cyril Genik had come to be considered by many settlers as "something of a czar of Canada."

In February 1999, in Winnipeg, a plaque was unveiled to commemorate the invaluable role that Cyril Genik had played in the settlement and strengthening of the Ukrainian community in Canada.

CHAPTER 3

Charting a New Course

Frank Oliver

Frank Oliver's appointment as Minister of the Interior and Superintendent General of Indian Affairs on 8 April 1905 heralded significant changes in Canadian immigration policy. Although Oliver (1853–1933) and Clifford Sifton were both Liberals and newspapermen adept at using the press to publicize their views, they differed markedly in their approach to immigration. Oliver had in fact been one of the sharpest critics of Sifton's policies, at one time denouncing Slavic immigrants as a "millstone" around the necks of western Canadians.

Like Sifton, Oliver was a transplanted easterner who had headed west as a young man. Born of Irish and English origins in Peel County, Canada West, in 1853, he left high school to pursue a career in the printing trade. This took him first to Toronto, where he worked for the *Toronto Globe,* and then to Winnipeg, where he had a stint at the *Manitoba Free Press.* In 1876, he struck out by ox brigade from Winnipeg to Fort Edmonton, an isolated settlement

on the upper reaches of the North Saskatchewan River.

Edmonton became Oliver's home and it was here that the future parliamentarian founded the fiery *Bulletin,* his personal mouthpiece and Alberta's first newspaper. Between 1883 and 1896 Frank Oliver attacked the establishment as an independent Liberal, first in the Northwest Territories Council and then in its successor, the territorial legislature. Elected to the House of Commons in 1896, he became Minister of the Interior in 1905. He was appointed to this portfolio on the recommendation of Sifton himself, who, despite his personal dislike of the prairie pioneer, cited Oliver's "long service and capacity" when he suggested his name for the post.

Frank Oliver favoured a vigorous immigration policy, believing that Canada would benefit from a strong flow of immigrants. At the same time, the MP wanted to see the West settled by newcomers who shared the values and aspirations of established Canadians. Addressing the House on Commons on

Frank Oliver, Minister of the Interior and Superintendent General of Indian Affairs, 1905–1911.

> "We should exercise more prudence in the choice. What is fifty years in the life of a nation? It is nothing; and in building up our nation we should aim to have the best kind of men, men who would be prepared to maintain here the institutions of a free people. I do not at all agree with the principle that our one ambition should be to fill up the country."

the subject before he joined Wilfrid Laurier's cabinet, he said:

> The western prairies are the seat and cradle of the future population of this Dominion. They are the seat of power and control, and, as that population is, so will this Dominion be. If you fill those prairies with people of different ideas, different aspirations and different views from your own, you are simply placing yourselves under a yoke, you are swerving your country from that destiny which your fathers intended it, and which you fondly hoped you were achieving.

In Oliver's hierarchy of desirable settlers for the West, newcomers from eastern Canada, "our own people," occupied the top rung. British immigrants, who arrived as "ready-made citizens,"

ranked next, closely followed by Americans. Whether British immigrants came from rural Britain or from Britain's teeming towns and cities was of little consequence to Frank Oliver, who did not share Sifton's prejudice against immigrants from urban centres. Indeed, Oliver preferred Britons from the towns and cities to agriculturalists from central and eastern Europe. Canada could tolerate Britons who were not agriculturalists, but those "stalwart peasants in sheepskin coats" who violated the prevailing social mores were, for Oliver, altogether another matter.

Changing direction

No sooner had Frank Oliver become Minister of the Interior than he set about making immigration policy more restrictive. Two Acts capped his legislative program, the first being the

Immigration Act of 1906 and the second being the *Immigration Act* of 1910.

The Immigration Act of 1906

Besides defining "an immigrant," this Act barred a broad spectrum of individuals and increased the government's power to deport certain classes of immigrants. It also decreed the amount of "landing money" immigrants needed to have in their possession on arrival and provided for the establishment of controls along the Canada–United States border.

There had been laws since 1869 prohibiting certain kinds of immigration and since 1889 allowing designated classes of immigrants to be returned whence they came. The 1906 Act differed in degree, significantly increasing the number of categories of prohibited immigrants and officially sanctioning the deportation of undesirable newcomers.

The proposed Act inspired considerable debate in the House of Commons, much of it concerning the definition of an immigrant and the provision for a head tax on immigrants: a tax to be paid by each immigrant on being admitted to Canada. Sweeping aside all the technicalities, though, we find that this parliamentary discussion revealed two basic views about the general direction that immigration should take.

Among those who felt that immigration barriers should be raised was the provincial chief of the Conservatives, Frederick Monk, who thought that Canada should emulate the example of the United States and impose a head tax on immigrants. The son of an English Canadian father and a French Canadian mother, but a man more French than English in outlook, Monk said:

We should exercise more prudence in the choice. What is fifty years in the life of a nation? It is nothing; and in building up our nation we should aim to have the best kind of men, men who would be prepared to maintain here the institutions of a free people. I do not at all agree with the principle that our one ambition should be to fill up the country.

By contrast, W.M. German, the Liberal member from Welland, lobbied for an open-door policy:

The United States wanted to fill up their country with people and they did so; we want to fill our country with people…. Let the people come. They may not in all cases be desirable but we will endeavour to lead them in the proper paths and make them desirable when we get them here.

Not surprisingly, German's stance on immigration found favour with Canadian industrialists, who lobbied for a continuous stream of immigrants willing to work long hours for low pay. The ebullient Sir William Van Horne, archetypal capitalist and Canadian Pacific Railway president (1888–1899) was one such industrialist. Voicing chagrin over the new direction taken by Canadian immigration policy, Sir William stated bluntly:

What we want is population. Labour is required from the Arctic Ocean to Patagonia, throughout North and South America, but

the governments of other lands are not such idiots as we are in the matter of restricting immigration. Let them all come in. There is work for all. Every two or three men that come into Canada and do a day's work create new work for someone else to do. They are like a new dollar. Hand it out from the Bank and it turns itself in value a dozen or more times a year.

The Immigration Act of 1910

The second milestone in restrictive immigration legislation was reached in 1910. The *Immigration Act* of 1910, unlike the 1906 Act, conferred on the Cabinet the authority to exclude "immigrants belonging to any race deemed unsuited to the climate or requirements of Canada." The Act also strengthened the government's power to deport individuals, such as anarchists, on the grounds of political and moral instability.

Although its exclusionary provisions were drastic and the discretionary powers it conferred on the Cabinet

Immigration Branch certificate for Mah Chew Wah, who paid $500 for the Chinese head tax, June 1921.

Citizenship and Immigration Canada Historical Collection

virtually unlimited, the Act of 1910 did not provoke a heated and prolonged debate in the House. While the Act inspired more discussion (some of the discussion focussed on the conspicuous failure of the government to address the immigration needs of the Maritime provinces) than had its predecessor, there was no major disagreement with its principles. As William Scott, Superintendent of Immigration from 1908 to 1924, later observed,

The discussion which took place upon the bill showed that Canada, in common with other young countries, whose natural resources attract the residents of the over-crowded communities of Europe, is fully aware of sifting 'the wheat from the chaff' in the multitudes who seek her shores.

Following passage of the Act in 1910, a $500 head tax was imposed on immigrants of Asiatic origin, a formidable sum for those days when it is realized that the average production worker in Canadian manufacturing took home only $417 in annual wages in 1910. An Order in Council in the same year levied a tax on all immigrants, the figure varying according to the season of the year. This last tax ignited a storm of protest in Great Britain because it required that each immigrant, male or female, have $25 in addition to the ticket or funds that he or she would need in order to travel to a predetermined destination in Canada.

Cancellation of the North Atlantic Trading Company contract

When details of the government's secret agreement with the North Atlantic Trading Company were revealed in Parliament in 1905 (a payment to the company for each agriculturalist it directed to Canada: see chapter 2), the Conservatives bitterly condemned the scheme. The opposition's attack and his own desire to trim the number of newcomers from continental Europe persuaded Frank Oliver to cancel the agreement the following year. Although he was prepared to be less selective about British immigration, the minister wanted to move in the opposite direction where continental European immigration was concerned. In the future, if "Sifton's pets" wanted to emigrate to Canada, they would have to do so on their own initiative.

Organized labour, of course, welcomed this attempt to curb immigration from southern, central, and eastern Europe. Fearing the impact of surplus workers on unionization and Canadian wage levels, the labour movement had routinely denounced contract labour schemes and government-assisted immigration. There was more involved, however, than the desire to protect jobs. In these years, workers of British descent harboured a deep dislike of newcomers from eastern, central, and southern Europe, a dislike that they shared with a majority of middle-class Canadians. This hostility was no more graphically expressed than in the pages of the *Toronto Tribune,* a trade-union publication of the day. In 1906, the paper reacted to the arrival of thousands of central and southern Europeans that year with a stinging observation: "The commonest London loafer has more decency and instincts of citizenship than the Sicilian, Neapolitan, Croat or Magyar." Echoes of these sentiments would later find expression in the fulminations of labour leader S.R. Berry, who in 1910 protested to Frank Oliver about "the sudden influx of immigrants whose habits of life and moral characteristics are repugnant to Canadian ideals."

Although the North Atlantic Trading Company contract was consigned to the garbage heap of history in 1906, Oliver continued to apply Sifton's policy of paying booking agents to recruit suitable immigrants. In fact, he not only retained the policy, but extended it. Less than four months after the agreement was cancelled, the Department of the Interior began to pay selected European booking agents a bonus for farmers, gardeners, carters, railway surfacemen, navvies, and miners.

Promoting British immigration

In the wake of the cancellation of the North Atlantic Trading Company contract, Frank Oliver took steps to bolster British immigration. Canada, he claimed, had to reinforce its British heritage if it was to become one of the world's great civilizations. Accordingly, the minister raised the bonus paid to British booking agents who sold tickets to British farmers, farm labourers, and domestics, and had new immigration offices opened in Exeter, York, and Aberdeen. The following year, 1907, the Immigration Branch adopted an even more aggressive approach to immigrant recruitment, appointing 100 government agents and paying each one a two-dollar bonus for every British agricultural labourer recruited and placed in Ontario or Quebec.

Immigration from the British Isles soared from 86,796 in the fiscal year ended 31 March 1906 to 142,622 in the fiscal year ended 31 March 1914. Although there is no conclusive evidence, one can probably attribute part of this increase to the bonuses awarded British shipping and Canadian government agents. The immigration figures disclose, for instance, that while the United States received over four times as many British immigrants as did Canada in 1900–1, the United States admitted approximately 7,000 fewer immigrants than did the Dominion in 1906–7.

The Vancouver Riot of 1907

In the course of promoting British and American immigration, Frank Oliver moved further along the path of selective immigration. Several developments conspired to push him in this direction, one being the Vancouver Riot of September 1907. The riot, which resulted in extensive damage to buildings occupied by Orientals, was precipitated by a rock hurled by a youngster through the window of a Chinese store following a giant anti-Asian parade.

Although the rampage ignited spontaneously, it had complex origins. The riot's principal roots lay deep in an anti-Asian sentiment that had been smouldering for years in British Columbia. This racial antipathy reached new heights in 1907 when it was reported that the Grand Trunk Pacific Railway was planning to import thousands of Japanese labourers to work on the completion of the railway's western leg. To add to the tension, over 2,300 Japanese arrived in the province in July alone, far more than had been anticipated.

With Japanese immigration soaring to unprecedented levels, the perception grew among West Coast whites that the Japanese had become the leading Oriental threat to their province's cultural integrity. The Japanese, like the Chinese, had always been regarded as unassimilable, but after Japan's victory over Russia in the Russo–Japanese War (1904–5) the Japanese image took on an even more frightening dimension. A growing number of white British Columbians now regarded the Japanese immigrant as aggressive, loyal first to Japan, and eager to further that country's expansionist aims.

As alarm mounted over the Japanese influx, hysterical comment about the Japanese "invasion" appeared in the daily press. Accompanying these expressed fears were demands by the Vancouver Trades and Labour Council for measures to stem the rising immigrant tide. Not content to work within the political process alone, the council formed the Asiatic Exclusion League. The league subsequently broke all ties with the Trades and Labour Council and staged the anti-Asian parade that preceded the Vancouver Riot of 1907.

Following the riot, the Laurier government found itself in the seemingly untenable position of having to placate British Columbia and Japan simultaneously. The solution lay in compromise. In response to British Columbia's insistent demands that Asian immigration be halted, Ottawa negotiated an agreement with Japan whereby Japan would voluntarily limit the emigration of Japanese to Canada to 400 a year.

As part of this same initiative, the government dispatched Mackenzie King, the Deputy Minister of Labour and a future Prime Minister, to Vancouver to investigate and settle Japanese claims for damages. In his capacity as a one-man Royal Commission, King conducted a series of

Adrienne Clarkson:
Governor General

Prime Minister Jean Chrétien summed up the significance of Adrienne Clarkson's appointment as Canada's first immigrant Governor General when he said on 8 September 1999, "Her appointment is a reflection of the diversity and inclusiveness of our society and an indication of how our country has matured over the years."

The celebrated broadcaster, writer, publisher, and former Ontario diplomat was only three years old when the Poy family—she, her parents, and a schoolboy brother—arrived in Montréal from Hong Kong, only to be told that they could not enter Canada because they were Chinese. It was 1942, the world was at war, and in refusing them entry the immigration officials cited the *Chinese Immigration Act* of 1923, whose broad provisions virtually banned the admission of all Chinese to Canada.

Fortunately, the officials were prepared to listen to Mr. Poy's unusual story. He told them that it had been arranged that he be allowed into Canada with his family under the terms of a Japan–U.S. prisoner swap, although he was neither Japanese nor a prisoner. When the story checked out, the family was allowed into the country. Greatly relieved, they headed straight to Ottawa, which would become their new home.

Ambitious, disciplined, and highly intelligent, Adrienne made a name for herself at Ottawa's Lisgar Collegiate Institute, where she became head girl during her graduation year (1955–56), excelled as one of the school's top students, and finished second in a Rotary Club public-speaking contest during her final year.

After graduating from Lisgar, Adrienne studied English literature at the University of Toronto, obtaining a master's degree in 1961. Further post-graduate work followed at the Sorbonne in Paris (1962–64), where she perfected the French that she had learned in Ottawa.

Canada's 26th Governor General acquired her first public profile as a pioneer in Canadian television. Between 1965 and 1982, she worked on the CBC programs *Take Thirty*, *Adrienne at Large*, and the *Fifth Estate*. As one of television's first female stars, she was noted for her intelligent and intense style.

In addition to working as a TV journalist, Ms. Clarkson has served as a diplomat. From 1982 to 1987, she won high praise for her work in Paris as Ontario's Agent General. Following her return to Canada she became the president and publisher at McClelland and Stewart (1987–88) and then publisher of Adrienne Clarkson Books for that firm (1988). She is the author of *Love More Condoling* (1968), *Hunger Trace* (1970), and *True to You in My Fashion* (1971).

At the time of her appointment as Governor General, Adrienne Clarkson was Chairman of the Board of the Canadian Museum of Civilization in Hull, Quebec, a position that she had held since 1995.

hearings and then awarded $9,000 in compensation to Japanese victims of the Vancouver Riot. Chinese riot victims, who had sustained more damage, later received $26,000.

Once the Japanese claims were settled, Mackenzie King sought to determine the origins of the recent Oriental influx. In his report, he attributed the abnormally large numbers to high immigration from Hawaii and to the activities of immigration companies based in Canada. King concluded that immigration by way of Hawaii should be banned, that companies should be prohibited from importing contract labour, and that Ottawa should severely limit the admission of Japanese newcomers. He also implied that immigration from India should be discouraged.

In response to King's findings, the Laurier government made an important amendment to the *Immigration Act.* This amendment, which came into effect in 1908, was known as the "continuous-journey regulation." Under this regulation, all would-be immigrants were required to travel to Canada by continuous passage from their country of origin or citizenship on a

through-ticket purchased in that country. Since no shipping company provided direct service from India to Canada, this ingenious device served to ban all Indian immigration. It also closed the door on the Hawaii route for Japanese immigration.

The Komagata Maru incident

The continuous-journey regulation and subsequent barriers to East Indian immigration did not go unchallenged. The most dramatic challenge occurred on 23 May 1914, when 376 East Indians (22 were returning Canadian residents) arrived in Vancouver harbour on board the *Komagata Maru,* a Japanese tramp steamer hired by a wealthy Sikh merchant and former labour contractor from Hong Kong, Gurdit Singh Sarhali. The steamer met with an unmitigatedly hostile reception. In fact, for weeks the vessel lay in harbour, its human cargo deprived of food and water by Canadian authorities who sought to weaken their resolve.

Finally, on 20 June, in the face of impending starvation, a passengers' committee agreed to the Canadian

government's demand that a test case go before an Immigration Board of Enquiry. A week later the case of Munshi Singh, a young Sikh farmer, was heard and he was ruled inadmissible on the grounds that he had violated three Orders in Council, in particular the continuous-journey regulation. When the B.C. Court of Appeal upheld the refusal of a lower court to order his release, the way was paved for Munshi Singh and all the remaining passengers to be deported. This happened exactly two months after the arrival of the doomed ship in Vancouver harbour. With the local citizenry cheering from the docks, Canada's *HMCS Rainbow* escorted the *Komagata Maru* to international waters. The steamer then sailed to India, having left behind just a handful of passengers, previous residents of British Columbia who had been allowed to land by the federal government.

Sikh political pressure finally persuaded the federal government to pass an Order in Council in 1919 allowing "British Hindus residing in Canada" to bring their wives and children to this country. The detested continuous-journey regulation remained in effect, however, until 1947.

Establishment of a border inspection service

In his attempt to make Canadian immigration policy more restrictive and selective in comparison to Sifton's, Frank Oliver, in 1908, instituted an immigration inspection service at 37 points of entry along the Canada–United States border in the Central Canada District, which stretched from Toronto to Sprague, Manitoba.

The budget for the service was so tight in the early years of its operation that no provision was made for office accommodation or detention facilities. Hard-pressed immigration and customs officers (the latter also took on immigration duties) had to work under extremely trying conditions in depot waiting rooms, on ferry docks, and on railway platforms. And the work could be dangerous. In one incident, Border Inspector H.G. Herbert was shot to death on a Windsor–Detroit ferry by an individual who had been refused entry to Canada.

Theory and practice

Frank Oliver might have wanted his government to pursue a more restrictive immigration policy, but prevailing belief had it that Canada's prosperity required a large dose of immigration. No more influential exponents of this view could be found than employers of large numbers of immigrant labour, who wielded considerable influence in both the Laurier and Robert Borden cabinets.

Sikhs on board the *Komagata Maru*. The infamous *Komagata Maru* incident, May to July 1914, involved the arrival of 376 emigrants from India, who were barred entry into Canada despite the fact they all had valid British passports.

National Archives of Canada (C 38599)

So, despite the introduction of restrictive immigration legislation and head taxes, people continued to stream into the country. In 1906, the influx exceeded 200,000, and in 1911, the year that the Liberals were toppled from power by the Conservatives under Robert Borden, more than 300,000 people entered Canada. In 1913, the number of immigrants climbed to a record figure of 400,000.

Both the Liberal and the Conservative governments succeeded in dramatically reducing immigration from Asia, but they failed to block the flow from central and eastern Europe. The reason is not hard to find. It had been Ottawa's goal to attract good agricultural settlers to Western Canada, and in realizing this aim it created the need for immigrants of another kind. Settlers demanded railways, manufactured goods, grain elevators, and schools and services in towns and cities—demands that generated jobs. Businessmen and companies, in turn, needed and clamoured for a large pool of cheap labour.

The most culturally acceptable immigrants came from the United Kingdom and the United States, but they did not match the businessman's concept of the ideal malleable labourer. British and American newcomers were not prepared to tolerate, for example, the low wages or the wretched working conditions of railway construction. Furthermore, they were all too familiar with unions, which could pose a problem for employers.

An observation by Thomas Shaughnessy, who succeeded Sir William Van Horne as President of the Canadian Pacific Railway, reflected the attitude of many of his business associates:

> *Men who seek employment on railway construction are, as a rule, a class accustomed to roughing it. They know when they go to work that they must put up with the most primitive kind of camp accommodation…. I feel very strongly that it would be a huge mistake to send out any more of these men from Wales, Scotland or England…. It is only prejudicial to the course of immigration to import men who come here expecting to get high wages, a feather bed and a bath tub.*

By contrast, Asiatics were seen as ideal workers. The Chinese had demonstrated their worth as labourers during the construction of the CPR, where they were assigned some of the most backbreaking and dangerous work. However, the wholesale importation of Asiatic labourers was out of the question because of the restrictive legislation enacted against Asian immigrants.

Canadian industrialists therefore turned increasingly towards central and southern Europe for the semi-skilled and unskilled labourers needed to supply the goods and services required by the new settlers. Of the continental Europeans, the Ukrainians were the most acceptable to Canada's industrialists and the Immigration Branch. Although they had proven to be good agriculturalists, the Ukrainians were prepared to work for wages and under conditions that other nationalities would not tolerate. Moreover, they were already pouring into the country. An estimated 63,425 Ukrainians entered Canada between 1891, when the first wave of Ukrainian immigrants arrived, and 1905, when Frank Oliver joined the Laurier Cabinet. Another 59,000 Ukrainians arrived during Oliver's term as Minister of the Interior.

Creating a new society

Between 1896 and 1914, some three million newcomers settled in Canada. Between 1901 and 1911, when the Canadian population rocketed by 43 percent, the percentage of foreign-born in the country as a whole exceeded 22 percent. Almost overnight, it seemed, immigration from Great Britain, the United States, Europe, and Asia had transformed the country, particularly Western Canada, into a polyglot society.

The transformation was not without its tensions, however. As has already been noted, public debate raged over the assimilability of those immigrants who spoke an incomprehensible language, who practised a strange religion, and who lacked a grounding in even the fundamentals of parliamentary democracy. The spectacle of bloc settlements in rural areas of the Prairies and the appearance of crowded ethnic ghettos in Canada's rapidly growing cities disturbed most English Canadians; they came to feel that it was their duty to help these foreigners transform themselves into the English Canadian ideal,

"making them clean, educated and loyal to the Dominion and to Great Britain."

Among those Canadians who took up the "Canadianization" cause in earnest were Methodists and Presbyterians. James Shaver Woodsworth (1874–1942) was one such individual. A well-known Methodist minister, social reformer, and pacifist, Woodsworth played a distinguished role in nearly all the reform movements of the pre-First World War era, and later became one of the founding leaders of the Co-operative Commonwealth Federation, the forerunner of the New Democratic Party.

Woodsworth's concerns about the assimilability of eastern, central, and southern European immigrants were sharpened by his experience with newcomers in Winnipeg's North End in the early years of this century. Living and working in the heart of that foreign world, where pigs and chickens roamed the unpaved streets and the infant mortality rate was shockingly high, Woodsworth came to believe that if immigrants were to become good Canadians they had to embrace Anglo-Canadian Protestant values and become

part of a Christian society in English-speaking Canada.

In his well-known work *Strangers within Our Gates,* published in 1909 when he was superintendent of All People's Mission in Winnipeg's North End, Woodsworth argued:

> *We, in Canada, have certain more or less clearly defined goals of national well-being. These ideals must never be lost sight of. Non-ideal elements there must be, but they should be capable of assimilation. Essentially non-assimilable elements are clearly detrimental to our highest national development, and hence should be vigorously excluded.*

He believed, in other words, that immigration should be controlled when it caused social problems or conflicted with what were perceived to be the goals of national life, and that all immigrants admitted to Canada should be capable of being assimilated into mainstream Anglo-Canadian society. For Woodsworth, as for most of his compatriots, the principal instruments of

Canadianization were the public schools. As he expressed it,

"The public school is the most important factor in transforming foreigners into Canadians." He maintained that "too great emphasis cannot be placed upon the work that has been accomplished and may—yes, must—be accomplished by our National Schools."

English-speaking Canadians were not the only group alarmed by the transformation that Canada's population was undergoing. Many French Canadians also voiced misgivings about what was happening, claiming, for example, that Ukrainian immigrants were a threat to Canadian institutions. As immigration figures climbed to new heights, these observers wondered what the future of French Canadians would be in the West, where French Canadians were beginning to be outnumbered by several other ethnic groups, and in Canada overall, where the relative size of the French-Canadian population was declining.

Henri Bourassa (1868–1952) was the barometer for many of the concerns of these French Canadians. During his first years in Parliament the celebrated journalist and politician supported Sifton's immigration program, but when he realized that immigration was shifting the balance of Canada's population and threatening to reduce French Canada's influence, Bourassa began voicing Quebec's opposition to the huge influx of foreigners into the West. One such occasion arose during the 1906 session of Parliament, when he observed:

When all was said and done, however, immigration was helping Canada realize several of its goals. Tens of thousands of successful farmers were rapidly transforming the Prairies and fuelling a booming economy; countless unskilled and semi-skilled newcomers were providing the back-breaking labour necessary to construct railways, build bridges, and extract ore from mines.

So many immigrants arrived from continental Europe in the years immediately preceding the First World War that the Anglo-French consensus that had dominated the social, political, and cultural life of nineteenth-century Canada was permanently altered. Although most noticeable in the Prairie provinces, the newcomers also had a decided impact on society in the rest of Canada. In this sense they heralded the dramatic changes that immigrants would introduce to post-Second World War Canada. Before that second buoyant period of immigration, however, lay the First World War and three decades of immigration doldrums.

CHAPTER 4

Immigration Slump

Prime Minister Robert Borden.

National Archives of Canada (PA 28128)

For Canada, the period between the turn of the century and 1913 involved years of unbounded hope and large visions. The population grew at an unparalleled rate. Between 1901 and 1911 it increased by more than a third, from 5.3 million to 7.2 million, thanks chiefly to immigration. Vast stretches of the Prairies were settled, two transcontinental railways were built with generous public assistance, and industrial production increased dramatically. In fact, during the so-called Laurier boom, from 1896 to 1913, Canada's average rate of population growth towered above that of any other country, including the United States. It is no wonder that Prime Minister Laurier predicted in 1904 that "the Twentieth Century shall be the century of Canada and of Canadian development."

Prospects for continued unabated growth began to dim, however, in the year that the tide of immigrants crested. In 1913, the country started to slide into a severe depression that would prove far worse than the short, sharp recession of 1907. The expansion of the economy and the growth of industry had depended on a continuous supply of liquid capital, but in 1913 this dried up. With the disappearance of capital, industrial expansion went into reverse and unemployment figures soared, especially in urban areas.

The First World War

The worrisome economic depression was bad enough, but a greater disaster lay just ahead: the First World War. The crisis that erupted in the Balkans in the summer of 1914 initially appeared no more ominous than half a dozen of its predecessors, but inexorably alliance systems solidified and mobilization plans were put into action. Serbia, Russia, and France were pitted against the German and Austro-Hungarian empires. With the expiration of the British ultimatum to Berlin at midnight on 4 August 1914, another empire went to war.

When Britain declared war on Germany on 4 August, Canada was automatically at war as well, an arrangement that most of its population enthusiastically supported. Across the country, Canadians sang patriotic songs in

British immigrants prior to their departure for a new life in Western Canada, circa 1920. Following the First World War, the Canadian government undertook immigration measures that distinctly favoured British immigrants.

The First World War claimed the lives of 60,661 Canadians, one-tenth of the more than 600,000 soldiers who went to war. Approximately 60,000 returned hopelessly maimed in body or mind. In Canada itself, the conflict widened the breach between English and French Canadians, particularly after the Conscription Crisis of 1917, which also destroyed the unity and esprit de corps of both the Liberal and Conservative parties. But if the war claimed many Canadian lives and created internal political unrest, it gave a tremendous boost to Canadian industry. Canada became modernized through the effort it put into mobilizing and equipping a huge army. Even more important, the war marked the real birth of Canada and its recognition by countries around the world.

Thrust upon the world's stage, Canadians performed well and often brilliantly. In late April 1915, the First Canadian Division, badly outnumbered and choked by gas, held the line at the Second Battle of Ypres, thereby averting a German breakthrough. Summing up his feelings about that horrendous

the streets, and the Minister of Militia and Defence was deluged with thousands of volunteers, eager to fight and confident that the imperial forces would soon prevail and that hostilities would be of short duration. No one at that time, not even the most pessimistic public official or private citizen, could foresee that the war would drag on for years and so seriously test the resources and unity of the country. No one could have predicted the ultimate consequences of Prime Minister Robert Borden's pledge

> *"to put forth every effort and to make every sacrifice necessary to ensure the integrity and maintain the honour of our Empire."*

Forging our Legacy

battle, the promising French-Canadian politician Talbot Papineau wrote:

"Some reports are appalling. I should feel dreadfully if they are true, yet what a glorious history they will have made for Canada. These may be the birth pangs of our nationality."

———

Two years later, in April 1917, Canada's name rang around the world after all four divisions of the Canadian Corps accomplished what had seemed impossible, the capture of the imposing Vimy Ridge, henceforth a symbol of Canadian achievement and pride. This heroic feat was followed by the Corps' grim victory at Passchendaele later that year and, in 1918, by its pivotal role in helping to crush the Germans in the final days of the conflict.

Canada's sacrifices and accomplishments on the field of battle transformed it—in military terms if not in constitutional law—from a colony into a sovereign nation. When Prime Minister Robert Borden affixed his own signature to the peace treaties in 1919, he set the seal on Canada's newly won status.

This status was reinforced when Canada, along with the other dominions, not only acquired separate membership in the League of Nations but also the right to separate election to the League's council and separate membership in the International Labour Organization.

Far less obvious as consequences of the war were the post-war achievements of individual Canadians who had served overseas, achievements that helped to shape the new Canada. Almost all of the soldiers who had survived the ordeal on the blood-soaked western front asked themselves why they and not their fallen comrades had been allowed to live. In their quest for an answer, many consciously set out to promote the Canadian spirit through their own endeavours and develop the kind of institutions that would serve as memorials to those who had died overseas. Lester B. Pearson is perhaps the best known of this particular category of survivors. He became a peacemaking diplomat who, against many odds, secured the United Nations' first peacekeeping force to oversee the Anglo-French (and a simultaneous

Israeli) withdrawal from Egypt during the Suez Crisis of 1956. For this remarkable achievement he won the Nobel Prize for Peace. He later went on to become Prime Minister.

More than anything else, Canada's participation in the First World War contributed to the country's development of a sense of distinct nationhood. The blossoming of cultural nationalism in the 1920s was one manifestation of this new attitude. Toronto was the centre of the movement, which found expression in *The Canadian Forum* (established in 1920), an independent journal of opinion and the arts, and the work of the Group of Seven (officially founded in 1920), whose bold depictions of the rugged and harsh North gave birth to a new image of Canada.

Cultural nationalism would gain further strength in the 1930s, when Canadians took important steps to protect and nurture their own identity. The most significant of these was the founding of the Canadian Radio League (later the Canadian Broadcasting League), whose purpose was to promote national broadcasting in Canada. Lauded by Graham Spry, one of its founders, as "a

Nobel Peace Prize winner Lester B. Pearson with Paul Martin Sr., while Prime Minister Louis St. Laurent looks on.

National Archives of Canada (PA 114542)

majestic instrument of national unity and national culture," the CRL lobbied for legislation that would result in the establishment of the Canadian Broadcasting Corporation. In 1933, only a year after the founding of the Canadian Radio League, the Dominion Drama Festival was inaugurated, and in 1939 the world-renowned National Film Board had its beginning. All three institutions would play invaluable roles in helping to shape and preserve Canadians' sense of identity.

If the First World War encouraged the growth of Canadian nationalism, it also heralded the growth of anti-foreign sentiment and the advent of several precipitous declines in immigration. In 1915, the year after hostilities erupted in Europe, immigration plunged to 36,665, the lowest figure since 1898, with three-quarters of this number arriving from the United States. The following year, immigration increased to 55,914, and in 1917, to 72,910. Then the number skidded to 41,845 in 1918, the year that the war ended. The following year it soared to 107,698.

The First World War and foreign-born Canadians

Besides slowing down the movement of newcomers to Canada, the First World War created difficulties for many foreign-born Canadians. Germans, who had previously ranked high on the list of desirable immigrants, were not the only ones to suffer. Deemed "enemy aliens" because they had once been citizens of Germany or of the Austro-Hungarian Empire, Hungarians, Czechs, Romanians, Poles, and Ukrainians also experienced hardship as a result of the war.

Although these people had freely settled in Canada and were contributing to this country's economic and social development, the Canadian government regarded them as a potential problem. Colonel Sam Hughes, the

Rosalie Silberman Abella: Outstanding Public Servant

German-born jurist Rosalie Silberman Abella has chalked up many impressive accomplishments over the years. In the process she has received 17 honorary degrees, become a Fellow of the Royal Society of Canada, and earned a reputation as one of Canada's most tireless advocates for the fair and equal treatment of its citizens.

Born in Stuttgart, Germany, in 1946 to Holocaust survivors, young Rosalie Silberman embarked for Halifax with members of her family on an American troop ship in May 1950. Not yet four years of age, she was officially a displaced person, one of 250,000 displaced persons and other refugees who were admitted to Canada between 1947 and 1962.

The ship carrying her family, the *General Heintzelman*, docked at Pier 21, from 1928 to 1971 the point of entry at Halifax for many immigrants to Canada. From Pier 21, she, her younger sister, her parents and her grandmother boarded a soot-filled train for Toronto, where they would start their lives all over again.

Within days of arriving in Toronto, her father, a lawyer, approached the Law Society of Upper Canada to ask what tests he had to write to become a lawyer in Ontario. None, was the reply. Non-citizens could not become lawyers. Since Jacob Silberman had a family to feed he could not wait the five years necessary to qualify for citizenship. He therefore became an insurance agent.

Recalling this chapter in her family's saga, Judge Abella said in 1999, "The moment I heard that story as a child about my father not being able to be a lawyer, was the moment I decided to become one. But as I grew up, people told me that girls were not lawyers. Not so, said my parents. This is Canada. With hard work anything is possible."

Thanks to hard work, Rosalie Silberman Abella obtained a BA from the University of Toronto in 1967 and an LLB from that university in 1970, two years after her marriage to historian Irving Abella. She practised civil and criminal law from 1972 until 1976, when, at the age of 29, she was appointed to the Ontario Family Court, becoming Canada's first Jewish woman judge.

Rosalie Abella, who describes herself as "a cautious optimist," served as a member of the Ontario Human Rights Commission from 1975 to 1980 and as an Ontario Family Court judge from 1976 to 1987. She was the sole commissioner on the 1983–84 federal Royal Commission on Equality in Employment, which created the term and concept of employment equity. Between 1984 and 1989 she chaired the Ontario Labour Relations Board. In 1992, she was appointed Justice of the Ontario Court of Appeal, which position she still holds.

Judge Abella has been a visiting professor in the law faculty at McGill University and a senior fellow at Massey College. She has also written four books and more than 70 articles. She and Prof. Abella have two sons—Jacob, born in 1973, and Zachary, born in 1976.

When she arrived in Canada 49 years ago, Rosalie Silberman Abella was presented with a precious gift—the possibility of endless possibilities, as she phrases it. Her life and career demonstrate that she has indeed made the most of that possibility.

tempestuous and bungling Minister of Militia and Defence, even went so far as to suggest that native-born Germans, Austro-Hungarians, and others of enemy-alien extraction should "be encouraged to go to the United States." Many Canadians were unsympathetic to their plight, having come to regard "foreigners," especially German immigrants, with apprehension and distrust, if not outright hostility.

Unsubstantiated rumours of imminent invasions of Canada by large forces of German-Americans and alarming reports of suspicious activities in the German-American communities of several American cities increased Canadian anxiety about foreigners in their midst. This uneasiness was further heightened by an incautious statement made by a Winnipeg prelate, Bishop Nykyta Budka. On 27 July 1914, while the world anxiously awaited Austria's response to the assassination of the Archduke Francis Ferdinand, the bishop urged his Ukrainian parishioners to remember their duty to the Austro-Hungarian Empire if war should occur and to hasten to the defence of the threatened fatherland.

The bishop affirmed his loyalty to the British Empire in a second pastoral letter, but his initial statement was not soon forgotten.

In the early months of the war, Robert Borden's Conservative government urged Canadians to adopt an attitude of tolerance and restraint towards enemy aliens. Nevertheless, harassment of enemy aliens not only continued but intensified as the conflict dragged on. Southwest of Toronto, in Berlin, Ontario, a prosperous city where persons of German ancestry made up three-quarters of the population, anti-German feeling ran so high that a statue of Kaiser Wilhelm was pulled down and heaved into the lake in Victoria Park. In 1916, the city's name was changed to Kitchener.

While it might have encouraged restraint on the part of the citizenry, the government itself began interning enemy aliens in camps across the country at the outbreak of hostilities, thereby removing political and labour activists from the public arena. Later it instituted vigorous censorship of the foreign-language press, banned a number of "foreign" organizations, and

prohibited groups that employed enemy languages from meeting.

The *Wartime Elections Act*, invoked in the 1917 federal election, was perhaps the most extraordinary measure taken against enemy aliens. In addition to giving the federal vote to women in the armed forces and to the wives, sisters, and mothers of soldiers in active service (Canadian women as a whole had not yet won the right to vote in federal elections), the Act withdrew this right from Canadians who had been born in enemy countries and had become naturalized British subjects after 31 March 1902. To become naturalized, each immigrant had had to bring an application for naturalization before a court official and swear an oath of allegiance. The court official, on being satisfied that the applicant was of "good character" and had fulfilled a three-year—five-year after the passage of the *Naturalization Act* in 1914—residency requirement, would then have issued a naturalization certificate. Like native-born Canadians, these naturalized immigrants were subjects of the British Crown, not Canadian citizens, because British nationality, or British

George Ignatieff: Peacemonger

George Ignatieff (1913–1989), one of Canada's most celebrated diplomats and a man devoted to the cause of peace, was among the comparatively small number of Russian newcomers who landed on Canadian shores in the 1920s.

Ignatieff, whose father was a famous Russian aristocrat, was born in St. Petersburg on 16 December 1913. Within a few brief years, the Russian Revolution and civil war had put an end to his sheltered childhood and the wealth and privileges enjoyed by his family. His public-spirited and highly respected father, once an education minister under the Czar, was arrested and jailed in 1918 by the Bolsheviks, but then was miraculously released in time for the family to escape to England.

In England, the neophyte émigrés operated a dairy farm. Young George attended St. Paul's, a boarding school, until the sale of the farm forced the family to move once again. While his father tried to raise funds in Europe for Russian refugees, Mrs. Ignatieff set out in 1928 with George and his brother, Leonid, for Canada, where two other brothers of George's, Nick and Jim, had already settled.

Although there was barely enough money for basic necessities, George's resourceful mother managed to squeeze enough out of the household budget to send her young son to Montréal's exclusive Lower Canada College. The stock market crash of 1929, however, put an abrupt end to George's private-school education. With the advent of the Great Depression, Ignatieff and the rest of his family united under one roof in Thornhill on the northern outskirts of Toronto.

After graduating from Toronto's Jarvis Collegiate Institute, George Ignatieff enrolled at the University of Toronto as a student of political economy. This turned out to be a particularly fortunate move because at the university he was exposed to the innovative ideas and influence of Donald Creighton and Harold Innis, then the rising stars of Canadian political and economic history. From these two inspiring teachers Ignatieff gained, in his words, "an insight into both the unity and the diversity of the country, the need to balance its cohesive forces against its economic regionalism and the cultural duality of the founding races."

Graduation from the University of Toronto was followed by a stint at Oxford University as a Rhodes Scholar. George Ignatieff's time at Oxford coincided with the Spanish Civil War and the growing militarization of the Axis powers. To make sure that he was not misinterpreting what he believed were the portents of another world war, Ignatieff travelled as often as he could in Italy and Germany. Some chilling discoveries awaited him, especially at Nürnberg. There he was appalled by the sight of a sea of storm troopers parading in front of the Führer.

After the outbreak of the Second World War, George Ignatieff enlisted in the British army. He was still in the army when, at the urging of Lester B. Pearson, then serving at the Canadian High Commission in London, he wrote the examination for the position of third secretary in Canada's foreign service. His top standing in the exam landed him a post in Canada's Department of External Affairs in 1940.

As a civil servant, George Ignatieff developed an expertise in East–West relations, particularly at the United Nations, where he served as Canadian Ambassador from 1966 to 1969 and as President of the Security Council from 1968 to 1969. He also served as Ambassador to Yugoslavia from 1956 to 1958 and as Permanent Representative to the North Atlantic Treaty Organization (NATO) from 1963 to 1966. During the 1950s and 1960s Ignatieff participated in highly charged negotiations involving most of the world's hot spots—the Middle East, Suez, Korea, Czechoslovakia, Cyprus—and discussed disarmament with anybody who would listen to him.

After retiring from the Department of External Affairs, George Ignatieff served as Provost of Trinity College, University of Toronto, from 1972 to 1979 and as Chancellor of that university from 1980 to 1986. In addition to his work in higher education, he continued to champion the cause of disarmament, speaking frequently and eloquently on the subject.

"subjecthood," was then the basic identity of all peoples living under the British Crown.

Borden's Conservative government sought to justify the disenfranchisement of citizens of enemy-alien birth, but its motives remained suspect. In the words of one blunt-speaking Liberal Member of Parliament, the only ground upon which enemy aliens were being disenfranchised was that the government suspected them of committing "the high crime and misdemeanour of being liable to vote Liberal at the next general election."

The return of peace

Peace brought a renewal of immigration, but not at the levels of pre-war days. In fact, with the exception of a few years in the 1920s, Canada would not again receive substantial numbers of immigrants until the 1950s.

Recession, uneven prosperity, and the anti-foreign sentiment of the pre-war and war years all combined to create antipathy to immigration and to throttle the movement of newcomers to this country in the early post-war period. At war's end, the European economy was in a shambles and destruction was widespread. Canada could have responded to Europe's plight by opening its doors to the continent's homeless. Instead, this country erected one roadblock after another to discourage immigration from Europe.

Anti-foreign sentiment played no small role in this. Canadians, like their neighbours to the south, had succumbed to a "Red scare" following the Russian Revolution of 1917. As a result, they took a jaundiced view of Canada's accepting European immigrants, fearing that these newcomers would bring with them dangerous ideologies in addition to their foreign languages and strange lifestyles.

In any event, because of the widespread unemployment that came in the wake of the armistice in Europe, Canada was not about to welcome immigrants in large numbers. The unemployment rate had risen dramatically because the wartime demand for the products of Canadian industry had ceased, and the situation was only exacerbated by the rapid demobilization of Canadian servicemen. Inevitably, Canadians became increasingly disillusioned with a peace that had held such promise but that appeared to produce nothing but hardship.

Given these conditions, it is not surprising that many Canadians pressed for the dismissal of foreign workers to make way for Canada's war heroes. Leaders of business and industry went along with these sentiments, perhaps because they had their own agenda. Fearing that returned veterans would embrace socialism if they did not obtain immediate employment, various companies and employers' organizations declared that they would dismiss enemy aliens and offer their jobs to demobilized soldiers. The International Nickel Company, located in Sudbury, Ontario, was one such company, demonstrating where its sympathies lay by dismissing 2,200 of its 3,200 employees, the overwhelming majority of whom were foreigners.

The Winnipeg General Strike

The spiralling cost of living, widespread unemployment, and disillusionment with "the system" gave rise to a wave of labour unrest that rolled across the country in 1918 and 1919, intensifying fears of an international Bolshevik conspiracy. Nothing did more to inflame anti-foreign sentiment and heighten fears of revolution than the Winnipeg General Strike of May 1919.

This general strike, which was triggered by the refusal of employers to recognize the Metal Trades Council as the bargaining agent for its affiliated unions, succeeded in paralysing the city of Winnipeg and splitting it into two distinct camps. Caught up in the hysteria of the time, leading members of the city's establishment denounced the strike as a revolutionary conspiracy led by a small group of "alien scum." In making this charge, they completely ignored the fact that nearly all the strike's leaders were British-born and British-educated, and not central European Bolsheviks.

Ultimately, the decisive intervention of the federal government brought about an end to the conflict. Persuaded that enemy aliens had instigated the strike, the government succeeded in 1919 in amending the *Immigration Act,* to allow for their easy deportation. It

View looking east along Portage Avenue on "Bloody Saturday" of the Winnipeg General Strike.

National Archives of Canada (PA 163001)

then had ten strike leaders arrested and instituted deportation proceedings against the four who were foreign-born. When a protest parade on 21 June turned ugly, Royal North West Mounted Police charged the crowd, leaving one person dead and many others wounded. "Bloody Saturday," as it came to be called, led to the arrest and deportation of 34 foreigners and effectively broke the Winnipeg General Strike. But it would leave a long-lasting legacy of bitterness and unrest across Canada.

Minimizing ethnic diversity

The revised *Immigration Act* and the Orders in Council issued under its authority signalled a dramatic shift in Canadian immigration policy. Prior to the First World War, immigration officials had chosen immigrants largely on the basis of the contribution that they

Three immigrants of various ethnic backgrounds who settled in Canada in the early 20th century.

National Archives of Canada (C 9798)

peasants" of the Sifton era were not, unless, of course, their labour was in demand.

In June 1919, the federal government, reflecting the prevailing anti-foreign sentiment and influenced by the economic realities of the day, used the revised *Immigration Act* to bar entry to specified classes of immigrants. Among those to be denied entry to Canada were Doukhobors, Mennonites, and Hutterites, as well as all persons who then were, or during the war had been, enemy aliens.

In 1918, groups of Hutterites, driven north from the United States by anti-foreign sentiment, had established ten colonies in the Calgary and Lethbridge areas of Alberta and six in Manitoba west of Winnipeg. More hoped to follow, but in 1919 they, along with members of the other pacifist sects, were barred from settling in Canada. They continued to be unwelcome until June 1922, when the regulation was rescinded by the newly elected Liberal government of Mackenzie King.

Taking advantage of the government's now more tolerant view of

could make to the Canadian economy, whereas now they attached more

importance to a prospective immigrant's cultural and ideological complexion. As a result, newcomers from the white Commonwealth countries, the United States, and to a lesser extent the so-called preferred countries (that is, northwestern Europe) were welcomed, while the celebrated "stalwart unorthodox religious sects, some 20,000 Russian Mennonites put down roots in Canada between 1923 and 1929. Like their predecessors, these Russian Mennonites were exempt from military service, but unlike earlier Mennonite newcomers, they were not allowed to settle in blocs.

In 1923, the government finally abolished the head tax that since 1885 had been imposed on Chinese immigrants, only to replace it with a new *Chinese Immigration Act* whose exclusionary provisions were so broad that Chinese immigration was virtually banned. The new law went into effect on 1 July 1923, forever after dubbed "Humiliation Day" by Canadian Chinese. From that date until it was repealed in 1947, the Act succeeded in virtually suspending Chinese immigration to Canada.

British youth were among the groups that were actively recruited in the 1920s to boost agricultural development in Canada.

Canadian Pacific Limited (2053)

Courting British immigrants

When the economy became more buoyant in 1923, the federal government once again set out to court British immigrants. As they had in the past, immigration officials targeted Britons prepared to farm. To lure them to this country, Ottawa initiated several colonization schemes that provided transportation assistance and other inducements. Despite such measures, however, British immigration in the 1920s never reached pre-war levels, over the decade averaging approximately 54,000 persons a year compared with approximately 99,000 annually in the ten years preceding the First World War. Moreover, only a small number of those who immigrated from Britain in the 1920s went into agriculture.

A group of Jewish orphans who immigrated to Canada, 1927.

National Archives of Canada (C 42732)

Jewish immigration

Although immigration to Canada between 1919 and 1925 was largely restricted to newcomers from Canada's traditional source countries, there were two notable exceptions. One involved the Russian Mennonites, discussed above; the other, Jews. Even though the Department of Immigration and Colonization was generally hostile to the idea of admitting Jews, placing various impediments in their way, approximately 40,000 Jews did succeed in entering this country during the interwar period, most being admitted by special permit. Among these Jews were 200 war orphans who were brought to Canada in 1920 largely through the efforts of the well-known Ottawa merchant A.J. Freiman and his wife, Lillian, who used their influence to raise $150,000 for this purpose.

In 1923, the Canadian government agreed to admit 5,000 Jewish refugees who had fled from Russia to Romania between 1918 and 1920 and had subsequently been ordered to leave their adopted country; of this number, some 3,040 refugees actually arrived in Canada. When the Jewish community petitioned the government to substitute Jewish refugees displaced in other parts of Europe for the remaining allotment of 2,000, the government turned down their request, claiming that many of these people could not be considered genuine refugees because they had left Russia with the consent of the authorities.

The railway agreement

In 1919, the framers of Canadian immigration policy believed that, to meet the country's economic needs, sufficient numbers of white English-speaking agriculturalists and industrial workers could be obtained either in Canada or from the United States and Great

Britain. In arriving at this conclusion, however, they failed to take into account the sweeping changes in American immigration legislation that had sharply reduced the number of immigrants from continental Europe allowed to enter the United States. Nor did they take into account the absence of quotas on the entry to the United States of native-born Canadians and the inevitable outcome of such a policy— an increase in the numbers of Canadian agricultural and industrial workers flowing southward and a corresponding decrease in the Canadian labour pool.

When the exodus of Canadian workers assumed alarming proportions, Canadian industrialists and farmers joined transportation and mining interests in lobbying the federal government for a more liberal immigration policy. Clifford Sifton set the tone for the new immigration campaign when he declared in 1922 that 500,000 "stalwart peasants" were required in Western Canada. These people, he urged, should be brought immediately from "Central Europe, particularly from Hungary and Galicia."

In response to this pressure, the Mackenzie King government gradually removed most of the barriers erected against large-scale European immigration, starting in 1923 with the repeal of the regulation that restricted the entry of immigrants from Germany and its wartime allies. The real breakthrough came two years later when Ottawa signed an agreement with the Canadian Pacific Railway and the Canadian National Railways, allowing them to recruit cheap foreign workers under the guise of bona fide European agriculturalists. This paved the way for Canada to receive immigrants from countries previously designated "non-preferred" by immigration authorities, countries such as Latvia, Lithuania, Estonia, Poland, Russia, Yugoslavia, Germany, Austria, and Romania.

The Great Depression chokes off immigration

If the Railway Agreement of 1925 led to a surge in the influx of newcomers from continental Europe, the Great Depression of the 1930s succeeded in choking off almost all immigration to Canada. During these years of economic devastation and widespread unemployment, the federal government strove hard to seal off Canada not only to prospective immigrants but also to refugees fleeing Nazi Germany, particularly Jewish refugees.

The few notable exceptions to the new exclusionary policy of the R.B. Bennett Conservative government were agriculturalists with means, immediate relatives of Canadian residents, and British subjects and Americans who had sufficient capital to maintain themselves until they could obtain employment. Given such a policy, it is not surprising that immigration plummeted from 1,166,000 in 1921–31 to only 140,000 in 1931–41.

There can be no doubt that Ottawa's restrictive legislation reflected the general Canadian attitude towards immigration, for Canadians across the country took the view that immigrants threatened scarce jobs in an economy that in 1933 saw almost one-quarter of the labour force unemployed. Prospective immigrants as well as immigrants already established in Canada became the targets of opposition. Among those who felt the brunt of such hostility were foreigners employed on a reforestation project near North Bay, Ontario. In May 1931,

German-Jewish refugees fleeing Nazi Germany reach Montréal seeking a new home, 19 November 1938.

National Archives of Canada (PA 156125)

Deporting the unwelcome

All immigrants who had not lived in Canada long enough to obtain domicile (five years for non-British subjects and one year for British subjects) and, ideally, citizenship[2] could be deported if they got into trouble or no longer held a paying job. This provision of the *Immigration Act* was a weapon frequently used throughout the "hungry thirties" to relieve municipalities, employers, and the state of unwanted foreign workers who had become surplus, useless, or obstreperous. Between 1930 and 1935, an estimated 30,000 immigrants were summarily deported, largely for being a public charge. Their ejection from Canada did not fail to arouse the sympathy of concerned Canadians, however, and government deportation officers themselves were among those most distressed by their plight. At least two officers serving in the western region became severely depressed and one later committed suicide.

they roused the ire of local residents, who claimed that Canadian workers had "to stand around and starve while foreigners get the first privilege."

[2]All non-British subjects had to be naturalized before they could obtain citizenship, which allowed them to vote in elections, etc. In order to qualify for naturalization, whose requirements were spelled out by the *Naturalization Act* of 1914, they had to be domiciled (that is, resident) in Canada for at least five years and be of "good character." By contrast, British subjects from other parts of the Empire—the British Commonwealth after 1931—were exempt from naturalization and required only one year of residence in order to qualify for the full rights of Canadian nationals.

Thomas Bata:
Shoemaker to the World

Few Europeans fleeing Nazi oppression in the 1930s managed to gain admission to Canada. One of the handful who did was Thomas Bata, the man who went on to build a global shoe empire that today employs thousands of people and plays an important role in the economies of many developing countries.

Born into a shoemaking family in Zlin, Czechoslovakia, on 17 September 1914, Thomas Bata was groomed from an early age to succeed his father as head of the Bata Shoe Company, then the largest shoe-manufacturing and shoe-retailing organization in the world. When Bata Senior died in an airplane crash in 1932, his son and only child was 17 years old. Ill-equipped to assume control of the number-one employer in Zlin, young Bata immediately set out to pursue studies at a commercial academy and to acquire additional managerial experience.

After graduating from the academy a year later, Thomas Bata became manager of the Bata shoe store in Zurich. As he was not yet 19, taking charge of one of the largest stores in the Bata organization represented a major challenge. It was nothing, however, compared to the challenges faced by the family business after the Munich Pact and the German invasion of Czechoslovakia in March 1938. With no wish to live under a Nazi regime, either temporarily or otherwise, Tom Bata fled to Switzerland and from there to England, where he sought permission to enter Canada and establish his shoemaking business with the aid of families recruited from Zlin.

Thomas Bata chose Canada because he believed that it incorporated the best of two worlds, or as he phrased it, "a blend of British traditions with the progressiveness and dynamism of the United States." Moreover, to a young man of 24, eager to flex his entrepreneurial muscles, Canada seemed to offer a more congenial environment than the highly industrialized United States.

The Depression of the 1930s had not yet released its grip, and gaining admission to this country was difficult. When it became apparent that Bata's entreaties alone were insufficient and that well-orchestrated pressure would have to be put on the Canadian government, the Canadian National Committee on Refugees, a volunteer organization, went to work. The result was a spirited press campaign and representations on behalf of the Bata Shoe Company from assorted boards of trade, county councils, and Belleville-area Members of Parliament.

In due course, Bata and 82 of his key Czech workers settled just outside of Frankford, Ontario, where they laid the groundwork for a business that would employ over 700 workers by the fall of 1940 and become an international success story in the post-war years.

When he was 75 years old, Thomas Bata experienced the thrill of standing on a balcony overlooking the town square of Zlin and receiving an exuberant welcome home. In the 50 years since he had left Czechoslovakia for Canada, his homeland had been subjected to first Nazi and then Communist rule before once again becoming a democratic republic. Bata, meanwhile, had become the chairman of a global shoe-manufacturing and shoe-retailing organization that employed 70,000 people in 73 countries.

The Liberal Prime Minister, Mackenzie King, had a genuine sympathy for refugees, but his sympathy took a distant second place to another consideration: keeping Canada united. Above all else, the Prime Minister was committed to maintaining Canadian unity, and this required that he not ignore political realities and the will of the majority. He told a delegation from the Canadian National Committee on Refugees that only a huge public outcry could bring about a liberalization of Canada's immigration policy, and he urged the committee to educate the general public about immigration.

Closing the door to refugees

Among those barred from entering Canada during the 1930s were thousands of desperate refugees, many of them Jews fleeing persecution at the hands of the Nazis. Two years after Canada introduced its new exclusionary immigration policy, the National Socialists seized power in Germany and began waging ruthless warfare against Jews and other minorities, such as pacifists, Communists, gypsies, and Freemasons. The persecution of the Jews was particularly savage, especially after the German invasion of Austria in March 1938.

Thousands of the Jews who managed to escape the Nazi tide sought refuge in Canada, but by and large their appeals were ignored. In 1938, this country stalled for months before accepting an invitation to a refugee conference at Evian, France, because it knew that attendance implied an interest in liberalizing immigration laws and admitting substantial numbers of Jews—and this the government was not prepared to do.

The Liberal Prime Minister, Mackenzie King, had a genuine sympathy for refugees, but his sympathy took a distant second place to another consideration: keeping Canada united. Above all else, the Prime Minister was committed to maintaining Canadian unity, and this required that he not ignore political realities and the will of the majority. He told a delegation from the Canadian National Committee on Refugees (CNCR) that only a huge public outcry could bring about a liberalization of Canada's immigration policy, and he urged the committee to educate the general public about immigration.

A number of political realities stayed his hand when it came to revising Canada's immigration regulations. One of these was the general perception that immigration threatened employment, and another was Quebec's attitude towards refugees in general and Jews in particular. Anti-Semitism was rife throughout Canada, where, in some places, Jews could not hold particular jobs, own property, or stay in certain hotels. It was most strident in Quebec, however, where right-wing, nationalist French-language newspapers castigated Jews and where some French-Canadian politicians and organizations denounced the idea of allowing Jews to seek refuge in Canada. In the face of such overwhelming anti-immigration sentiment, the Mackenzie King government maintained its policy of refusing to admit substantial numbers of Europe's oppressed.

Champions of the oppressed

As dismal as this picture appears, there were in fact many Canadians who opposed the government's policy and wanted to see immigration barriers lowered. In addition to members of pro-refugee organizations and leading spokespeople for the Jewish community, they included prominent members of the Protestant churches, newspaper editors and commentators in English-speaking Canada, and members of the Co-operative Commonwealth Federation, particularly its leader, M.J. Coldwell.

Foremost among the non-sectarian refugee lobbies was the Canadian National Committee on Refugees and Victims of Political Persecution, later shortened to the above-mentioned Canadian National Committee on Refugees. The committee was founded by the League of Nations Society in Canada, an organization of internationally minded Canadians dedicated to publicizing the work of the league and to persuading the government to adopt a pro-league stance. Spurred by European pogroms in the fall of 1938 and by the aftermath of the Munich settlement, which delivered a large chunk of Czechoslovakia to Hitler and prompted the flight of some 80,000 anti-Nazi resi-

Red Cross workers, a clergyman, and Canadian immigration officers welcome newly arrived European immigrants, circa the late 1940s.

Saskatoon Public Library - Local History Room

dents, the League of Nations Society mobilized for a new battle.

Under the leadership of Cairine Wilson, Canada's first woman senator, the CNCR devoted the next ten years to this struggle, educating the Canadian public about the plight of refugees, combating anti-Semitism, and assisting those refugees who succeeded in gaining entry to Canada. The committee also petitioned the government repeatedly for a more liberal immigration policy and for the admission of greater numbers of refugees.

Notwithstanding its energy and dedication, the committee remained small in numbers and ineffective in convincing the government to adopt a more humane immigration policy. Still, it played a valuable role in helping to settle individuals and families in

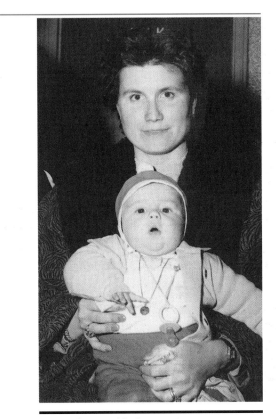

Mrs. Puliggi and baby Vittorio were among a group of 290 Yugoslav refugees from camps in Italy, Austria, and West Germany who arrived at the Port of Québec in April 1960.

National Archives of Canada (C 53922)

Canada and in raising public awareness of the refugee question.

The "accidental immigrants"

Perhaps the CNCR's most noteworthy contribution was the aid that it gave to some 2,500 anti-Nazi male civilians (Germans, Austrians, and Italians) who in the dark summer of 1940 were transported from Britain to Canada and then interned in Canadian prison camps. Owing to the efforts of committee members and individuals such as Saul Hayes, the leading spokesperson for the United Jewish and War Relief Agencies, conditions in the camps were improved and many internees were released before the camps were closed.

After the Second World War ended, in 1945, Canada reclassified these one-time prisoners as "Interned Refugees (Friendly Aliens) from the United Kingdom" and invited them to become Canadian citizens. Nine hundred and seventy-two accepted the invitation, thereby providing their adopted country with one of its most remarkable pools of foreign-born talent. Many—and the list includes Gregory Baum, Oscar Cahen,

and John Newmark—would go on to make outstanding contributions in fields as diverse as science, music, painting, theology, university teaching, literature, and the dramatic arts.

Guest children from Great Britain

The summer that saw civilian internees sent to Canada also saw an influx of British guest children arrive on Canadian shores. This was a time when the Germans were bombing Britain and invasion of the island kingdom seemed imminent. Many British parents decided that no corner of Britain was safe, and so they booked passages for their children on ships to Canada.

A stream of children crossed the Atlantic that summer of 1940, some of them participants in an evacuation scheme financed by the British government. All told, some 8,000 youngsters were shipped to Canada, almost 2,000 of them sent by the government-assisted program. The program was cancelled in September 1940 after the sinking of the *City of Benares,* with the loss of almost 100 children.

The plight of the Japanese Canadians

In Canada itself, probably no group of people experienced as much hardship and upheaval as the Japanese Canadians. Their ordeal began on 8 December 1941, the day after the Japanese bombed Pearl Harbor. Within hours of that attack, Ottawa ordered that fishing boats operated by Japanese-Canadian fishermen be impounded and that all Japanese aliens be registered with the Royal Canadian Mounted Police. The worst blow was delivered on 25 February 1942. On that day, Mackenzie King announced in the House of Commons that all Japanese Canadians would be forcibly removed from within a hundred-mile swath of the Pacific coast to "safeguard the defences of the Pacific Coast of Canada." Thus began the process that saw a visible minority uprooted from their homes, stripped of their property, and dispersed across Canada.

Relocation of Japanese-Canadians to camps in the interior of British Columbia during the Second World War, 1942–1945.

National Archives of Canada (C 46350)

Japanese Canadians, unlike their counterparts in the United States, were kept under detention until the end of the war. After the conclusion of hostilities, about 4,000 of them succumbed to pressure and left Canada for Japan under the federal government's "repatriation" scheme. Of these, more than half were Canadian-born and two-thirds were Canadian citizens.

The conclusion of the Second World War signalled the end of three decades of slow immigration and the subordination of humanitarian considerations to anti-Semitism and economic priorities. It also set the stage for a renewed interest in welcoming newcomers and a great upsurge in immigration.

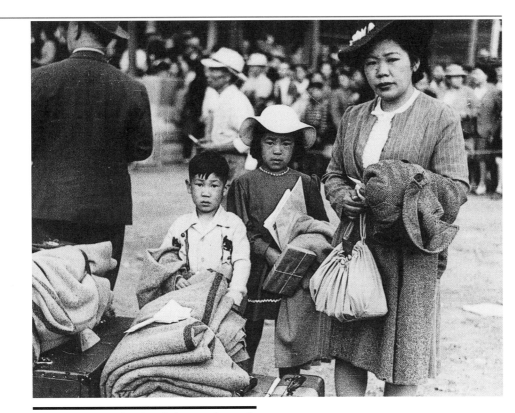

A Japanese-Canadian family being relocated to a camp in the interior of British Columbia during the Second World War, 1942–1945.

National Archives of Canada (C 46355)

CHAPTER 5

Towards the Canadian Citizenship Act

Liberal Cabinet Minister Paul Martin Sr.

National Archives of Canada (PA 47288)

The growth of Canadian nationalism

As it had after the First World War, Canada emerged after the Second World War with more self-assurance and confidence. There were good reasons for this. Despite having fewer than 12 million people, it had made a huge contribution in manpower and matériel to the Allied war effort and had developed a host of new and durable industries in the process. However, the cost of its participation in the war had been great: 43,000 men and women had died and the national debt had quadrupled. Yet casualties were much lower than they had been during the earlier conflict. Moreover, most of the wartime spending had been in Canada, resulting in the doubling of the gross national product.

The Statute of Westminster (1931) had accorded legal recognition to Canada's status as a self-governing dominion. A decade later, the Second World War confirmed Canada's place in the world. It also compelled this country to grow up technologically. Forced by wartime conditions to reduce their dependence on European and American goods, the leaders of the Canadian economy became far more daring, innovative, and self-reliant. As a result, the range and volume of Canadian industrial production increased dramatically. By war's end, the country's steel-making capacity had increased by more than 50 percent and Canadian factories were producing many items—aircraft, plastics, diesel engines, electronic equipment—that they had not made previously.

Although everybody had expected that the Second World War, like the First World War, would be followed by a severe recession, no such slump materialized. Instead, the country enjoyed a wave of prosperity. Initiated by wartime spending, it would last, with minor fluctuations, until the early 1970s, fed by a pent-up demand for consumer goods. Canadians had money in their pockets and they were eager to spend it. One by-product of Canada's new self-awareness in these buoyant years was a vigorous nationalism, which found expression in the *Canadian Citizenship Act* of 1947.

First Citizenship Ceremony, 3 January 1947.

National Archives of Canada (PA 197414)

The Canadian Citizenship Act of 1947

The vast majority of Canadians believed that the war had truly confirmed Canada as a sovereign nation and they wanted the rest of the world to recognize the country's recently won status. For that to happen, however, the remaining emblems of colonialism had to be removed and the symbols of independent nationhood substituted.

It would be a slow process. Not until 1949 would the practice of appealing decisions of Canada's Supreme Court to the Judicial Committee of the Privy Council in London be abolished; not until 1952 would this country acquire a Canadian-born Governor General; and it would be two decades before a distinctive Canadian flag made its debut. But one significant symbol of independent nationhood—Canadian citizenship—would find legal recognition in 1947, two years after the war. Up until that point, Canadian nationals had been legally defined as British subjects, both in Canada and abroad.

The credit for fathering the project that gave legal recognition to the term "Canadian citizen" goes to the Liberal Cabinet Minister Paul Martin Sr. The Minister first conceived the idea of a separate Canadian citizenship during the Second World War, but it was not until he visited the military cemetery at Dieppe after the war that the idea really seized hold of him. At Dieppe, while pondering the status of those who had served their country and were buried there, he resolved to incorporate into law a definition of what constituted a Canadian.

The deplorable state of Canada's naturalization laws added a note of urgency to his mission. Not only was there no such thing in law as a Canadian citizen; there were also ambiguities in the

Naturalization Act of 1914, the *Canadian Nationals Act* of 1921 (it provided a definition of "Canadian nationals," a requirement for Canadian participation in the League of Nations and membership in the International Court of Justice), and the *Immigration Act* of 1910, the three pieces of legislation that dealt with citizenship. The result, as Martin noted in Parliament, was unending confusion and embarrassment.

There were other anomalies. Married women, for example, did not have full authority over their national status. Classified with minors, lunatics and idiots "under a disability," they could not become naturalized or control their national status as independent persons, except in very special circumstances.

When introducing the bill relating to nationality and naturalization in the House of Commons on 22 October 1945, the Minister said:

Our "new Canadians" bring to this country much that is rich and good, and in Canada they find a new way of life and new hope for the future. They should all be made to feel that they, like the rest of us, are Canadians, citizens of a great country, guardians of proud traditions and trustees of all that is best in life for generations of Canadians yet to be. For the national unity of Canada and for the future and greatness of this country it is felt to be of utmost importance that all of us, new Canadians or old, have a consciousness of a common purpose and common interests as Canadians; that all of us are able to say with pride and say with meaning: "I am a Canadian citizen."

The *Canadian Citizenship Act,* which was enacted on 27 June 1946 and came into force on 1 January 1947, provided for the conferring of a common Canadian citizenship on all Canadians, whether or not they had been born in Canada. Canadian citizenship, however, was deemed a privilege to be granted only to those considered qualified.

Among the changes introduced by the new Act were the following:

- All Canadian citizens would have automatic right of entry to Canada.

- As a rule, immigrants (including those from the Commonwealth) would not qualify for full citizenship until they had been resident in Canada for five years and had taken out citizenship papers. However, immigrants who were already British subjects would not lose their existing rights, including the right to vote after they had resided in Canada for only one year. Immigrants who had served in the Canadian armed forces during the First or the Second World War would qualify for naturalization after only one year.

- Married women would be given full authority over their nationality status.

- Citizenship would be lost under certain circumstances, such as the adoption of citizenship of another country.

- Provision would be made for instruction in the rights and responsibilities of citizenship and for appropriate citizenship ceremonies, including a revised oath of allegiance.

- An applicant for citizenship could substitute 20 years of residence in Canada for a knowledge of English or French.

With the enactment of this revolutionary piece of legislation Canada became the first Commonwealth country to create its own class of citizenship separate from that of Great Britain. Henceforth Canadian citizenship could be acquired by immigrants who had been naturalized in Canada, non-Canadian British subjects who had lived in Canada for five or more years, and non-Canadian women who had married Canadian citizens and who had come to live in Canada.

In a moving and historic ceremony, staged on the evening of 3 January 1947 in the Supreme Court of Canada chamber, 26 individuals were presented with Canadian citizenship certificates. Among them were Prime Minister William Lyon Mackenzie King, who received certificate 0001, and Yousuf Karsh, the internationally acclaimed Armenian-born photographer.

Post-war rise in immigration

Not surprisingly, the *Canadian Citizenship Act* of 1947 coincided with a post-war rise in immigration. This upsurge in immigration did not follow immediately on the heels of the war, however. Proponents of a more liberal immigration policy had wanted to see Canada lower its immigration barriers as soon as the hostilities ended, but Canadian immigration policy continued to be highly restrictive in the first year or two after the war. Although it could have been a land of hope and promise for Europe's war-weary and oppressed, Canada admitted few bona fide immigrants and displaced persons (the label given to those individuals who had been uprooted or displaced in their own homeland by war) during this period. Immigration barriers also blocked the entrance of most refugees (people who had fled totalitarian regimes before the outbreak of the war and those who, starting in 1945, had left East European countries that had come under Communist control).

No matter what their designation—refugee or displaced person—all these people were essentially refugees without

a country, home, material possessions, or future, and their plight aroused the concern of increasing numbers of Canadians. Despite the demands of these compassionate observers for a more humane immigration policy, however, Canada's doors remained virtually closed to new arrivals. To justify its inflexibility, the government frequently cited a lack of suitable passenger vessels to transport people from Europe to Canada. Still, a few did make it.

Notable among the new arrivals to Canadian shores in the early post-war period were British war brides who had married members of Canada's fighting forces. During and after the war, some 48,000 of them arrived in this country, often with tiny babies in their arms and toddlers clinging to their skirts. Although most of the war brides and their approximately 22,000 offspring settled in Canada's towns and cities, some of them made their homes in rural or remote regions of this vast land.

Eventually, the requirements of this country's booming economy, a call from the Senate's Standing Committee on Immigration and Labour for a more open immigration policy, and mounting pressure from ethnic organizations, religious groups, transportation companies, and returning diplomats who had seen first-hand conditions in Europe forced the government's hand. In reaction to all these pressures, Mackenzie King's Liberal government began to slowly open the doors to Europe's homeless.

Polish war veterans admitted to Canada

Polish war veterans were among the first beneficiaries of Canada's tentative move towards a more liberal immigration policy. They were admitted after the government passed an Order in Council in July 1946 providing for the admission of some 3,000 Polish Free Army veterans who refused to be repatriated from Great Britain to a homeland occupied by the Red Army. Each veteran was bound by contract to serve on a farm for one year, after which he was free to renew or discontinue the contract. When their term was up, the majority of workers chose not to continue this arrangement and headed for Canada's cities in search of better-paying jobs.

Polish soldier immigrants arriving on the *Sea Robin* in Halifax, Nova Scotia, 12 November 1946.

National Archives of Canada (PA 111595)

Mackenzie King makes a statement on immigration

On 1 May 1947, in response to those who advocated a more liberal immigration policy, Mackenzie King made the following declaration in the House of Commons:

The policy of the government is to foster the growth of the population of Canada by the encouragement of immigration. The government will seek by legislation, regulation, and vigorous administration, to ensure the careful selection and permanent settlement of such immigrants as can advantageously be absorbed in our national economy.

Before concluding his oft-quoted speech, however, King stressed that

Displaced person (from Second World War) who emigrated to Canada and worked at Dionne Spinning Mills, St-George, Beauce County, Quebec, 21 May 1948.

National Archives of Canada (PA 115767)

immigration should not be allowed to "make a fundamental alteration in the character of our population." In other words, Asian immigration would continue to be restricted while applicants from the "old" Commonwealth countries and the United States would continue to receive preferred treatment.

Nevertheless, in deference to the United Nations Charter, the *Chinese Immigration Act* of 1923 would be repealed and Chinese residents of Canada, not already Canadian citizens, would be allowed to apply for naturalization.

King's statement paved the way for hundreds of thousands of Europeans to enter Canada in the next decade. For the first time since the turn of the century, a Canadian government had decided to use immigration as an instrument to boost the Canadian population and economy. Today, we would not consider this a bold move, but at the time it rep-

resented a dramatic shift in direction. Indeed, we can now see it as a watershed in Canadian immigration policy. For since that time Canada has made it possible for immigrants seeking a better life or refugees fleeing political or religious persecution to gain admission.

Canada opens the gates to displaced persons

To its credit, Canada decided to admit displaced persons even before the international community had reached an agreement on the permanent resettlement of hundreds of thousands of Europe's homeless. Taking independent action, this country passed an Order in Council in June 1947 authorizing the entry of an initial 5,000 non-sponsored displaced persons. Subsequent Orders in Council, passed between July 1947 and October 1948, provided for the entry of an additional 45,000 of these people, many of whom later sponsored European relatives. For several years Canada admitted more displaced persons (Canadians soon learned to call them "New Canadians") than all the overseas countries combined—far more, for example, than the United States.

Nearly 250,000 displaced persons and other refugees were admitted to Canada between 1947 and 1962. Of the 165,000 refugees who entered this country between 1947 and 1953, Poles comprised the largest group (23 percent of all those refugees admitted). In descending order of numerical strength were Ukrainians (16 percent), Germans and Austrians (11 percent), Jews (10 percent), Latvians (6 percent), Lithuanians (6 percent), Magyars (Hungarians; 5 percent), Czechs (3 percent), Dutch (3 percent), and Russians (3 percent). All told, these groups comprised 86 percent of the Europeans allowed to enter Canada in this period.

Five mobile immigration teams were dispatched to Germany and Austria in the summer of 1947 to select prospective immigrants. Composed of immigration, medical, security and labour officials, these teams travelled from one displaced persons' camp to another, interviewing many desperate people and living out of suitcases or, where possible, the trunk of a car. In a sense they resembled itinerant "head hunters," although their mission was to select able-bodied refugees. Preference was given to strong young men who could perform manual labour in Canada's primary industries, which at that time were experiencing an acute labour shortage.

These immigration teams were later lauded by Dr. Hugh Keenleyside, the Deputy Minister of the Department of Mines and Resources (immigration was then one of its responsibilities) from 1947 until 1949 and a key figure in the resettlement of displaced persons in Canada. Addressing an audience at Dalhousie University in November 1948, the highly respected Keenleyside praised the work of these early immigration officers and then observed:

> I think it is not an exaggeration to say that the achievement of bringing to Canada something over 50,000 D.P.s between July 1947 and November 1948 under the conditions that existed in Germany during that time, and in spite of the transportation difficulties which had to be overcome, is as remarkable a performance as anything to be found in the history of immigration to Canada.

Immigration of Balts to Canada

Because they ranked high on the list of Canada's preferred immigrants, Balts were among the first displaced persons selected by Canadian immigration teams dispatched to United Nations-run camps in Austria and Germany. Generally speaking, the Balts were Estonians, Latvians, and Lithuanians who had found themselves caught between Soviet and German forces in the Second World War. They had had to endure the 1940 Soviet occupation of their respective countries, the subsequent German invasion, and the advance of Russian forces in 1944.

When the Russians moved towards Estonia in 1944, thousands of Estonians fled their homeland by sea for Sweden and Germany. Of those who remained in Estonia, some later effected a dramatic escape to Canada. Between 1948 and 1950, almost 1,700 Estonians made their way independently by small, often unseaworthy, boats to Canadian ports, where ad hoc immigration machinery was set up to process them. The Canadian government admitted nearly all of these intrepid,

Lambertus Vandenberg and his family arrived in Ottawa via the SS *Volendam* from Holland to Québec City, 27 June 1949.

Jack Vandenberg Collection

would-be immigrants. Large numbers of other Estonians, usually displaced persons, would follow the "boat people" to Canada over the next few years, but their transportation and entry would be far more conventional.

Canada welcomes Dutch farmers

In an attempt to increase the population of Canada's rural areas, the Canadian government signed an agreement with the Dutch government that brought Dutch families to this country. Holland had been left with a surplus of farmers after retreating German soldiers had destroyed the country's dykes, leaving much of Holland's agricultural land flooded. Between 1947, when this immigration movement got under way, and the end of September 1949, nearly 16,000 members of Dutch farm families entered Canada. Many of these newcomers went to Ontario, but substantial numbers also settled in Quebec, Alberta, Manitoba, and British Columbia. The movement was so successful that the Immigration Branch continued to encourage farmers from the Netherlands to emigrate to Canada throughout the 1950s.

Contract labour

Canada's need for additional workers to serve the unquenchable needs of its expanding economy led the government, in 1947, to establish a program that encouraged companies to adopt "contract" or "bulk-labour" schemes. Many displaced persons who entered Canada in these years did so under this program. Potential employers in the mining, logging, or lumbering industries would forward applications to the

Department of Labour requesting that a certain number of labourers be brought to this country under pre-arranged contracts covering wages and basic living conditions. Shortly after its introduction, the program was expanded to include other types of labourers as well as specialized agricultural workers, such as the sugar beet farmers who settled with their families in Western Canada.

The legendary C.D. Howe, an American immigrant, an engineer, and the principal architect of the Canadian war effort, was one of the leading boosters of the contract-labour program. When Canada was converting to a post-war economy, Howe, who often represented the interests of the Canadian Manufacturers' Association in Cabinet, became an outspoken advocate of increased immigration, including the immigration of displaced persons. As Minister of Reconstruction and Supply and Acting Minister of Mines and Resources, he directed a steady stream of requests to Cabinet for the admission of skilled and unskilled European workers—craftsmen for the clothing industry, workers for heavy industry, lumber camps and construction, woodworkers, and people who could perform domestic work in homes, hospitals, and similar institutions.

Although the bulk-labour movement was successful in supplying badly needed manpower to Canadian industry and the resource sector, it did not lack critics. The sentiments of many of these were summed up in a 28 May 1947 editorial in the Toronto *Globe and Mail,* which assailed the government for a bankrupt immigration policy and roundly criticized it for allowing a Quebec Liberal, Ludger Dionne, to "import" a hundred Polish girls to work in his rayon mill. Huffed the *Globe,* "Instead of a bold, imaginative, large-scale plan for bringing them [people] in, the Government offers paltry schemes allowing employers to recruit labour on a plan of semi-servitude...."

From a different end of the political spectrum, representatives of the Canadian labour movement and the Co-operative Commonwealth Federation (the forerunner of the New Democratic Party) denounced the program because they believed that it would undercut wages and threaten to displace Canadian workers from their jobs. Alluding to press reports of Ludger Dionne's labour scheme, the Saskatchewan school teacher and CCFer Gladys Strum observed:

> *I do not think it improves our standing in the united nations [sic] to have appearing in our daily papers reports which sound like descriptions of scenes from* Uncle Tom's Cabin, *which remind one of the old slave market where girls were put up at auction with someone looking at their muscles and someone looking at their teeth.*

Despite the heated attacks against it, the bulk-labour movement did not begin to lose momentum until after U.S. President Harry Truman prodded Congress into passing the *Displaced Persons Act* (1948), which made the United States the preferred destination for many of Europe's homeless. This, coupled with the emptying of the camps in Europe, contributed to a downturn in immigration. When the Canadian labour market's insatiable demands could no longer be met, the government was forced to conclude that other means had to be resorted to—measures that would admit more people to Canada and at the same time ensure the right kinds of immigrants.

A further liberalization of immigration policy

The government responded, in June 1950, by issuing an Order in Council that replaced all former Orders in Council and amendments with respect to immigration; retained the preference for British, Irish, French, and American immigrants; and widened the admissible classes of European immigrants to include any healthy applicant of good character who had skills needed in Canada and who could easily integrate into Canadian society. Later in the year regulations were changed to allow the entry of additional categories of Asians. In a further move, the government took German immigrants off the enemy-alien list (Italian immigrants had been removed from the list in 1947). As a result, Germans joined swelling numbers of Italians in applying for admission to Canada.

Besides lowering immigration barriers another notch or two in 1950, the government established the Department of Citizenship and Immigration. No longer was immigration to be the responsibility of a multi-function department whose other activities bore little relation to immigration. Instead, it would be the responsibility of a new ministry, which had two major branches, the Immigration Branch and the Citizenship Branch. Such a move was considered essential if immigration was to receive the recognition and attention that it warranted.

By and large there was little general opposition to the increased movement of immigrants to Canada. Even organized labour, which had frequently opposed substantial influxes of newcomers in the past, raised little objection. In fact, it willingly assisted in the admission of new arrivals, especially displaced persons, and this despite the fact that these immigrants could compete for jobs. Probably the only trade union which officially and adamantly opposed the entry of qualified displaced persons was the Canadian Medical

Association, the major professional association of Canadian doctors.

There was also some shift in the attitude of Quebec's elites towards immigration. In the post-war years, Quebec academics and newspaper editorialists began to view immigration more positively, having come to realize that non-British immigrants had a great deal in common with French Canadians—both considered themselves Canadians first and British subjects second. Also, most eastern European newcomers had the additional advantage of being Roman Catholic, the religion of the overwhelming majority of French-speaking Quebeckers.

The 1952 Immigration Act

A long-awaited new *Immigration Act,* the first since 1910 (there had been significant revisions in immigration policy over the years, but no new *Immigration Act*) was finally enacted by Parliament in 1952. In many respects, the 1952 Act was similar to its predecessor. Nevertheless, in its major provisions it simplified the administration of immigration and defined the wide-ranging powers of the minister and his officials.

With respect to the selection and admission of prospective immigrants, the Act vested all-embracing powers in the Governor in Council (that is, the Cabinet). This meant that the Cabinet could prohibit or limit the admission of persons by reason of such factors as nationality, ethnic group, occupation, lifestyle, unsuitability with regard to Canada's climate, and perceived inability to become readily assimilated into Canadian society. An incriminating letter from Citizenship and Immigration Minister Walter Harris, written in 1952 but placed on record in the House of Commons in 1953 by CCF member Joseph Noseworthy, reveals all too clearly that these provisions were designed to exclude non-white immigrants.

One of the Act's most significant provisions vested a large degree of uncontrolled discretionary power in the Minister and his or her officials. This would have far-reaching, often negative, implications for Canadian immigration, but when it was used responsibly and creatively, it proved an invalu-

able tool in aiding desirable and/or humanitarian immigration.

Jack Pickersgill was one Minister who employed the Act compassionately and to good purpose. A flamboyant, fiercely partisan Liberal, who had abandoned an academic career for a stint in the public service and then politics, Jack Pickersgill used his ministerial powers to make fundamental changes in immigration policy when he was Minister of Citizenship and Immigration, from 1954 to 1957. On different occasions he waived immigration regulations and approved the admission, under minister's permit, of epileptics whose condition could be controlled by drugs, tubercular cases, and people who had a previous history of mental illness, provided these cases posed no danger to the community and were adequately sponsored.

Refugees from Palestine

When Pickersgill was at the helm of Citizenship and Immigration, Canada took the bold step of admitting some Palestinian Arabs, driven from their homeland by the Israeli–Arab war of

Citizenship and Immigration Minister J.W. Pickersgill with the Dean of Sopron University of Budapest, Montréal, Quebec, circa 1957.

National Archives of Canada (PA 147725)

1948. In 1955, when the idea for the scheme was conceived, over 900,000 Palestinian refugees were living in Syria, Lebanon, Jordan, and Gaza.

The resettlement of these refugees abroad was nothing if not a politically explosive issue in the Middle East. By participating in the operation Canada

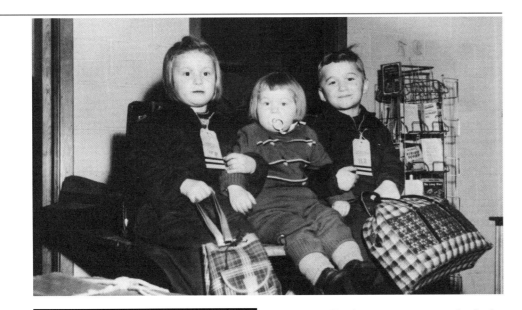

Hungarian children waiting in Rouyn-Noranda, Quebec, December 1956.

risked incurring the wrath of Arabs, who might charge that it was part of a Zionist plot to remove Palestinian refugees from the care they received from the United Nations Relief and Rehabilitation Administration and deprive them of their right to return to Palestine. Nevertheless, in 1955, a young official at the Canadian legation in Beirut, Lebanon, where UNRRA had its headquarters, approached the agency and obtained its co-operation in arranging for a selection of Palestinian refugees to be interviewed by a Canadian immigration team.

The following January, a Canadian immigration mission visited Lebanon and Jordan, and from among 575 applicants presented to it by UNRRA, chose 98 who were "apparently well qualified to become Canadian citizens." This number was eventually trimmed to 39 heads of families and their dependents and it was this group that departed for Canada in the summer of 1956. Much to the surprise of Canadian officials in Beirut, the undertaking did not trigger nearly as much opposition from Arab sources as they had anticipated.

The Hungarian refugees

In sharp contrast to the attention given its admission of the Palestinian refugees, Canada's admission of close to 38,000 Hungarian refugees in 1956–57 attracted a great deal of coverage over the years.

This country's response to the desperate situation of the Hungarian refugees represents one of the few times in Canadian history when Canadians have whole-heartedly welcomed immigrants. In fact, of all the states that accepted Hungarian refugees for permanent resettlement, none surpassed Canada in its generosity. The Louis St. Laurent Liberal government's speedy action and the generous admission program that it launched were not solely the result of government initiative, however. They can be attributed directly to the pressure created by the Canadian public, whose sympathies were aroused by the plight of over 200,000 Hungarians fleeing their homeland after

Russian tanks brutally crushed the Hungarian uprising in 1956.

On 6 November 1956, Jack Pickersgill instructed the Canadian immigration office in Vienna, Austria, where most of the Hungarians had fled, to assign top priority to applications from those Hungarians wishing to emigrate to Canada. While signalling Canada's recognition of an urgent situation, however, he did not waive or alter any of the normal immigration procedures and provisions.

Many Canadians, including members of religious and ethnic groups, the opposition parties (the CCF and the Progressive Conservatives), and newspaper editorialists, viewed this rather cautious approach as not enough. Pressure steadily mounted outside the government for a more energetic response. It was not long in coming. Immigration procedures were simplified, and in the last week of November Pickersgill initiated steps to charter a ship and aircraft to bring the first influx of refugees to Canada. Then the real breakthrough came. On 28 November, two days after Parliament convened in a special session to debate the Hungarian and Suez situations, the Minister announced that Ottawa intended to proceed with a generous admission program, whose chief feature was free passage for all those Hungarian refugees who met this country's admission standards.

After the House of Commons adjourned on 29 November, Jack Pickersgill flew to Vienna to take charge of the situation. There, assuming the role of "commandant," he made a number of important on-the-spot decisions to facilitate movement of the refugees.

In addition to masterminding the movement and settlement of thousands of Hungarians, the government also had to cope with 108,989 British immigrants spurred to emigrate by the Eden government's inept handling of the Suez crisis, which had erupted just before the Soviet invasion of Hungary. To handle the tens of thousands of Europeans and Britons heading for Canada, the Canadian government eventually launched an airlift program designated the "Air Bridge to Canada" or the ABC scheme. During the opening months of 1957, over 200 chartered flights brought nearly 17,600 immigrants to Canada, many of them young Hungarians. Indeed, the movement of Hungarians to Canada contained a predominance of young people.

These young Hungarians included a sizeable group from the Faculty of Forestry at the University of Sopron, some 350 students, families and professors. As the first group of this kind to emigrate to Canada, they travelled in a "freedom train" from Halifax to Vancouver, eliciting rousing receptions at stops all across the country. Thanks to initiatives taken by Pickersgill, the Forestry Faculty was incorporated into the University of British Columbia, where it functioned as the Sopron Division of the Faculty of Forestry until 1961. The members of another group, this one from the University of Sopron's Faculty of Mining Engineering, were assimilated into a variety of faculties at the University of Toronto.

In carrying out the resettlement of the Hungarian refugees (approximately one-third were settled west of the Great Lakes, one-third in Ontario and the remainder in Quebec and the Maritimes), the Department of Citizenship and Immigration succeeded in overcoming many restrictions in the system.

In the years ahead, the lessons learned would prove invaluable to immigration authorities, allowing them to respond more quickly and with greater flexibility to both refugee and ordinary immigration movements.

The downturn in immigration

Although there was a downturn in the Canadian economy in 1957, immigration to Canada that year was higher than in any year since 1913–14, totalling 282,164. While the influx of Hungarians and Britons contributed significantly to this figure, other factors were also at work, including the burgeoning numbers of sponsored immigrants (immigrants brought to Canada by relatives who could provide for their lodging, care, and normal settlement needs) and Ottawa's aggressive promotion of unsponsored immigration (that is, immigrants who applied for permanent residence in Canada on their own merit and who usually had skills of use to the Canadian economy).

As the Canadian economy became more and more sluggish, the newly elected Progressive Conservative government, which had assumed power in 1957, turned off the tap. As a result, immigration dropped off sharply. In 1958–59, the number of people immigrating to Canada plunged to 124,851; the following year, the number dropped again, to 106,928. Not until 1962 did it move upward again, one year after British immigration had skidded to its lowest level since the Second World War.

The new wave of immigrants

Unlike the newcomers in the earlier boom period of Canadian immigration (1900–1914), those who arrived in the late 1940s and 1950s were a more heterogeneous body, with a greater diversity of skills, training, and occupations. They arrived in a country much changed since the days when, in the picturesque phrases of the Senate Standing Committee on Immigration and Labour, the early immigrants had "laid axe to tree or struck long furrows in the Middle West." By 1957, the year that marked the end of the post-war boom period in Canadian immigration, Canada, which now included Newfoundland, boasted a population of 16,610,000 and ranked as a major industrial nation, with manufacturing providing its major source of income and employment. It was therefore the urbanized and industrialized provinces —Ontario, Quebec, Alberta, and British Columbia—that benefited most from immigration.

During these years the United Kingdom and the United States continued to furnish Canada with large numbers of newcomers, but no longer were they the predominant sources of immigrants. Now the majority of new arrivals came from continental Europe, especially Germany, Italy, and the Netherlands.

Despite a lack of consensus in Canada about the desirability of immigration, there could be no doubt that it had made an invaluable contribution in the 1940s and 1950s to the size and quality of the Canadian labour force. It accounted for two-thirds of the labour force's increase between 1950 and 1955 and for almost half the total increase between 1950 and 1960. Moreover, many of the new professional and new skilled jobs were filled by immigrants— saving countless dollars in professional and educational training in Canada.

Ludmilla Chiriaeff:
Ballet Celebrity

As founding director of Les Grands Ballets Canadiens and its schools, Latvian native Ludmilla Chiriaeff (née Otzoup-Gorny) played a prominent role in establishing ballet in Quebec.

Born in Riga in 1924, she trained in Berlin, studying ballet under many distinguished teachers. Choreographer Michael Fokine, a family friend, had a particularly powerful influence on her artistic development. As a resident of Switzerland after the Second World War, she danced and choreographed for various companies and directed her own Ballet des Arts in Geneva (1949–1951).

In 1952, when still in her twenties, Ludmilla Chiriaeff immigrated to Canada. That same year, in Montréal, she established a ballet school and formed the Ballets Chiriaeff, a troupe of eighteen dancers. The company made its official debut on Radio Canada–CBC in 1952, where over the years to come it would perform in some 300 televised shows. The new company, in which Ludmilla Chiriaeff continued to dance, performed live on stage in 1955. Three years later, in 1958, it evolved into Les Grands Ballets Canadiens.

Before the Quiet Revolution of the 1960s forged a new Quebec, religious conservatives openly denounced ballet as an immoral activity. Notwithstanding this opposition, Chiriaeff succeeded in establishing Les Grands Ballets Canadiens as one of Quebec's major cultural institutions. The company would soon be acclaimed across Canada and abroad.

Chiriaeff choreographed many of the company's ballets, among them Suite canadienne (1957), Cendrillon (1962), and Pierrot de la Lune (1963). She received a number of awards over the years, including the Order of Canada (1972; Companion of the Order 1984), the Molson Prize (1986), the international Nijinsky Prize (1992), and the Governor General's Performing Arts Award (1993).

Ludmilla Chiriaeff remained the company's artistic director until 1974 and continued to direct its schools until 1992, when ill health forced her to retire. She died in Montréal in 1996.

CHAPTER 6

Trail-Blazing Initiatives

During the boom period, 1947–1957, immigration restrictions were gradually eased to admit not only unsponsored refugees and displaced persons but ordinary immigrants from a growing number of countries. This was always done, however, with a view to preserving the fundamental character of the Canadian population. Access from countries other than those that belonged to the "old" Commonwealth, the United States, and Europe was severely restricted, because the Liberals under Mackenzie King and his successor, Louis St. Laurent, were not prepared to abolish Canada's racist immigration policy. The nominal credit for banishing racism from Canada's immigration policy belongs to the Progressive Conservatives, who toppled the Grits in the federal election of 10 June 1957 after a 22-year absence from the government benches.

Initially, John Diefenbaker and the Progressive Conservatives did little to signal that they would introduce bold changes in immigration policy. True, during the election campaign the combative Saskatchewan lawyer had promised that under a Progressive Conservative government immigration would play a vital role in Canada's development. Referring to the 1952 *Immigration Act,* "the Chief" announced, "We will overhaul the act's administration to ensure that humanity will be considered and put an end to the bureaucratic interpretations which keep out from Canada many potentially good citizens." And in an interview in March 1958, the month his government was returned to office with an unprecedented number of seats, he confidently predicted that Canada's population would reach 40 million in the foreseeable future, provided the federal government pursued a vigorous immigration policy. Nevertheless, despite these and similar pronouncements to journalists and gatherings of ethnic groups, Diefenbaker did not assign top priority to immigration in his government's early years.

Ellen Fairclough

Perhaps because of the Progressive Conservatives' reluctance to take decisive action on immigration issues, the uninfluential Citizenship and Immigration

Ellen Fairclough, who in 1957 became the first woman to serve as a federal Cabinet Minister.

National Archives of Canada (PA 148646)

portfolio was assigned in May 1958 to someone Diefenbaker mistakenly thought would serve as a caretaker minister. This was Ellen Fairclough, the vivacious Member of Parliament from Hamilton, Ontario, who in 1957 had become the first woman to serve as a federal Cabinet Minister when the Prime Minister appointed her Secretary of State during his initial term in office. By profession a chartered accountant who owned her own accounting firm, Ellen Fairclough would preside over the fortunes of Citizenship and Immigration for four years and three months.

Unfortunately, Fairclough's political fortunes took a drubbing during her first two years in Citizenship and Immigration, largely because of problems triggered by a deepening recession and the large influx of unskilled sponsored workers and sponsored family workers without paid employment. Family sponsorship was undermining attempts to relate immigration more closely to labour-market requirements. Furthermore, when sponsored family members became a public charge, municipal welfare costs rose, creating some resentment. In March 1959, therefore, the government embarked on a brave attempt to curb the escalating sponsorship movement, made up largely of unskilled Italian relatives from southern Italy.

When the new regulation limiting sponsorship to immediate family members was announced a month later, both the Liberal opposition and Canada's ethnic communities objected strenuously. Especially vocal were Italian Canadians who were well represented in Mrs. Fairclough's own riding. Defending her government's action, the embattled Minister informed the House of Commons that the backlog of sponsored applicants had grown from some 77,158 as of 31 December 1955 to 131,785 as of 28 February 1959. From Italy alone, the numbers had soared from approximately 12,000 at the end of 1954 and 23,000 at the end of 1955 to about 63,000 as of 28 February 1959.

In the face of all the uproar and a lack of support in Cabinet, Mrs. Fairclough backed down and on 22 April 1959 rescinded the new regulation. Thoroughly intimidated by the furor that had been aroused, the Diefenbaker government abandoned any further thought of early legislative changes to immigration policy. In the autumn of 1960, it would announce its intention to produce a new *Immigration Act,* but then fail to do so.

With the rescinding of the regulation, the sponsored movement continued to mushroom. This continued until mid-1960 when it became evident that immigration from Italy would outstrip immigration from Great Britain for the third consecutive year. When confronted by this prospect, Mrs. Fairclough's department renewed its efforts to curb the growth of the sponsorship program. To reduce the numbers, it once again attempted to make administrative adjustments. The changes introduced achieved the desired results and remained in effect, with minor modifications, until 1964.

World Refugee Year, 1959–60

Although the battle over sponsored immigrants cost Ellen Fairclough much in the way of political capital, the spirited Minister was still prepared to tackle difficult issues and run political risks. In 1959–60, for example, she allowed tubercular refugees and their families to be admitted to Canada as part of this country's contribution to the United Nations-sponsored World Refugee Year. This was a courageous move, given the fact that Canadian enthusiasm for refugee immigration had abated considerably since the arrival of the Hungarians two years earlier. The presence of die-hard Communists and other undesirables in the Hungarian influx had done much to awaken anti-immigration sentiment across the country.

At first, the Minister resisted the idea of admitting desperate refugees to Canada, but eventually she changed her mind. By flexibly interpreting the regulations and making liberal use of her ministerial powers, Ellen Fairclough opened Canada's doors to 325 tubercular refugees and 501 members of their families during World Refugee Year. They were among a total of 6,912 refugees admitted that year, which saw 70 countries intensify their efforts to close down the world's refugee camps and rehabilitate countless thousands of despairing people without a country. The refugees who arrived in Canada

came from many parts of Europe, although the majority were Polish, Ukrainian, and Yugoslavian.

During her term as Minister of Citizenship and Immigration, Ellen Fairclough oversaw a steady improvement in the operation and procedures of the Immigration Service. Measured against this and her other accomplishments, however, was one of even greater significance—the long-overdue and radical reform that virtually abolished the "White Canada" immigration policy.

Canada abolishes its racist immigration policy

The reform was introduced to the public on 19 January 1962 when Ellen Fairclough tabled new regulations in the House that virtually eliminated racial discrimination as a major feature of Canada's immigration policy. Henceforth any unsponsored immigrants who had the requisite education, skill, or other qualifications were to be considered suitable for admission, irrespective of colour, race, or national origin, provided (1) they had a specific

The Honourable Ellen Fairclough, Minister of Citizenship and Immigration, gets a kiss from one of the refugees allowed into Canada during World Refugee Year, 1959.

National Archives of Canada (PA 181041)

job waiting for them in Canada or were able to support themselves until they found employment, (2) they were not criminals or terrorists, and (3) they did not suffer from a disease that endangered public health. Only one vestige of true discrimination remained and that was the provision that allowed

European immigrants and immigrants from the Americas to sponsor a wider range of relatives. This clause would be removed five years later, however, in the immigration regulations of 1967.

When the new regulations were implemented on 1 February 1962, Canada became the first of the three large receiving countries in international migration—the other two being the United States and Australia—to dismantle its discriminatory immigration policy. In 1975, the United States embarked on a similar course by introducing amendments to the *Immigration Act,* which came into effect in 1978. Australia abolished its White Australia policy in February 1973 by simply announcing that it would grant citizenship on conditions applying equally to all.

The new regulations tabled by Fairclough in the House of Commons before she left the Department of Citizenship and Immigration were foreshadowed by John Diefenbaker's cherished Canadian Bill of Rights (1960). Since the Bill of Rights had rejected discrimination by reason of race, colour, national origin, religion, or sex, the federal government could no longer justify selecting immigrants on the basis of race or national origin. Moreover, the long-standing discriminatory provisions now seemed anachronistic and untenable in an era when provincial governments were legislating against discrimination on the basis of race, religion, and origin in such areas as employment, education, and accommodation.

The government had decided that the new immigration policy should be embodied in regulations rather than in statutes because regulations can be implemented quickly, while a new and complex *Immigration Act*—something the Progressive Conservatives had been promising—must first be steered through Parliament and that takes time. This last point was alluded to by the noted Canadian immigration expert David Corbett, who greeted the new regulations enthusiastically. He congratulated Ellen Fairclough for placing "immigration policy in its proper context as part of foreign policy" and speculated that the new regulations were ahead of public opinion and more liberal than those the Minister could have obtained had she tabled a new *Immigration Act.*

Richard Bell, the decisive Progressive Conservative minister who succeeded Ellen Fairclough in the Citizenship and Immigration portfolio on 9 August 1962, was a true believer in immigration. Time and time again he tried to persuade his fellow MPs that immigration is a stimulus to the economy and a powerful tool in nation-building. His enthusiasm for the cause led him to suggest to a Toronto audience on 18 November 1962 that annual immigration should be increased to a rate equivalent to 1 percent of Canada's population. Under questioning in the House of Commons the next day, however, the Minister explained that he had made "no statement of new policy, but a simple statement of what are appropriate targets and objectives."

New policy or not, Richard Bell decided to inject new vigour into his department. In the face of continuing high unemployment and the Cabinet's anti-immigration stance, he instructed Citizenship and Immigration to oil the machinery and reopen the doors to immigration. Partly as a result of the steps taken to crank up operations, as well as an upturn in the Canadian economy, immigration figures began to rise. Richard Bell, the member from Ottawa-Carleton, had presided over a veritable resurrection.

The 1966 white paper

Despite Bell's initiatives, truly bold moves in policy had to await the Liberals' return to power. When they took office under Lester B. Pearson in 1963, the Canadian economy was undergoing significant change. Because of the quickening pace of technological innovation, certain acquired skills were becoming obsolete and workers needed periodic training to keep up. Furthermore, notwithstanding an improved economy, the unemployment rate was still unacceptably high. And perhaps not surprisingly, the largest component of the reservoir of unutilized labour consisted of unskilled and undereducated workers.

Realizing that these harsh economic realities had a bearing not only on worker training but also on immigration policy, Pearson's government instituted a sweeping review of all aspects of immigration. The resulting white paper on immigration, which was tabled in Parliament in 1966, noted that immigration had "made a major contribution to the national objectives of maintaining a high rate of population and economic growth." Nevertheless, to prevent an explosive growth in the unskilled labour force, the paper proposed that the government tighten up the sponsorship system and admit more independent immigrants (immigrants who applied on their own initiative and had skills required in the labour market).

The Liberals also instituted an important structural change: the establishment of the Department of Manpower and Immigration. It owed its creation largely to the government's concern about the shortage of skilled workers and a conviction that manpower development programs could play an important part in training workers required by Canada's expanding economy. The Pearson government believed that the dearth of skilled workers could be solved by an increase in the flow of skilled workers to Canada and by the

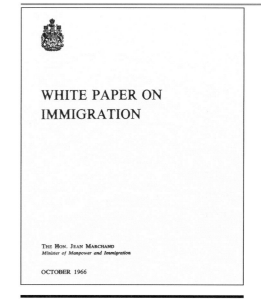

The 1966 white paper.

Citizenship and Immigration Canada Historical Collection

adoption of manpower development programs offering specialized training. One department, it was believed, should deal with both issues.

The points system

By far the most significant development in immigration policy in these years, however, was the introduction of the points system, a method designed

Robert Andras, Minister of Manpower and Immigration, 1972.

John Evans photographer

to eliminate caprice and prejudice in the selection of independent immigrants. In the points system, immigration officers assign points up to a fixed maximum in each of several categories, such as education, employment opportunities in Canada, age, the individual's personal characteristics, and degree of fluency in English or French. The points system was incorporated into

new immigration regulations that went into effect in 1967. Other features of these regulations included the elimination of discrimination based on nationality or race from all classes of immigrants and the creation of a special provision that allowed visitors to apply for immigrant status while in Canada.

Closely related to this last provision was the passage of the *Immigration Appeal Board Act* (1967), which set up a new and fully independent appeal board. Anyone who had been ordered deported could appeal to the board, no matter what his or her status was under the *Immigration Act*.

Now that visitors could apply for landed-immigrant status and there was the option of appealing to the Immigration Appeal Board (IAB), the numbers of people applying for landed-immigrant status increased dramatically. As a result, the effectiveness of the selection process abroad was seriously undermined and the appeal board was soon confronted by a staggering backlog of cases. Visitors who were refused landed-immigrant status invariably appealed to the board, confident that its case backlog would enable them to

enjoy the benefits of legally admitted immigrants for several years, and that whatever the result of their eventual appeal, by then the political pressure from the ethnic community and perhaps even the general public would make it extremely difficult for the government to deport them.

Robert Andras

During the first four years of Pierre Trudeau's administration, from 1968 to 1972, Ministers of Manpower and Immigration came and went with unseemly frequency. Such a rapid turnover did not augur well for a sweeping revision of Canadian immigration policy—and neither did the seriously troubled Canadian economy. Nevertheless, the Prime Minister paved the way for a dramatic and sorely needed overhaul of Canadian immigration policy when he appointed Robert Andras Minister of Manpower and Immigration in November 1972. Unlike his three immediate predecessors, Mr. Andras would oversee the production of not just a new *Immigration Act* but a radically new immigration statute. His remarkable achievement can be attributed to his determination to obtain a forward-looking new Act, his skills as a minister, and his strong voice in Cabinet. Moreover, he had the good fortune to take on the challenge at a time when there was a general recognition that change in immigration policy was long overdue.

A veteran of the Second World War, Robert Andras was president of four automotive sales and car rental firms when he was first elected to the House of Commons in 1965 as Liberal MP for Port Arthur (soon to be amalgamated with Fort William to create Thunder Bay). He would be re-elected four more times before retiring from politics in December 1979. Prior to taking on the Manpower and Immigration portfolio, he had held several Cabinet positions. Fittingly, his new appointment coincided with a period of rapidly increasing immigration. From 122,006 in 1972, immigration would climb to 184,200 in 1973 and then to 218,465 in 1974 before dipping to 187,881 in 1975 and 149,429 in 1976.

Andras lost no time in introducing reforms designed to prevent the government from losing further control over immigration policy. The most important of these was Bill C-197, which amended the *Immigration Appeal Board Act*. Assented to on 27 July 1973, it contained provisions designed to clear up the board's backlog of cases and to prevent the recurrence of the current crisis. Notable among these was the provision that abolished the universal right of appeal and that allowed only permanent residents of Canada, valid visa holders, and individuals claiming to be refugees or Canadian citizens to have a right of appeal to the IAB.

This provision was intended to address the problem for the long-term, but in the meantime the IAB still faced a staggering backlog of cases, over 17,000 at the end of May 1973. In the interests of immediate relief, Bill C-197 provided for establishment of the Adjustment of Status Program. Under this program persons who had lived in Canada continuously (legally or illegally) since 30 November 1972 and who had registered with an immigration officer within 60 days of the proclamation of the legislation could apply for permanent residence. An amnesty in all but name, the program was a conspicuous success, resulting in approximately 39,000 people obtaining landed-immigrant status.

The green paper of 1974

Although these reforms were important, they only laid the groundwork for a new *Immigration Act*. Radically new legislation was desperately needed as the realities of modern-day Canada had long since overtaken the *Immigration Act* of 1952.

Conceived essentially as a gatekeeper's act, the 1952 legislation focussed on the kinds of people who should be refused admission to Canada and outlined mechanisms for controlling the entry or visits of persons who had no legal right to be here or who were considered undesirable. It made no mention of the principles that should govern the selection of would-be immigrants nor did it reflect the fact that section 95 of the *British North America Act* (now known as the *Constitution Act, 1867*) recognizes immigration as a joint federal–provincial responsibility. In sum, it was riddled with shortcomings and should have been replaced years

Canadian Communist Party protesting the federal government's green paper on immigration policy, Toronto, 1975.

ago. Canada needed an *Immigration Act* that spelled out a coherent immigration philosophy and that took into account modern-day attitudes and practices, not to mention this country's immigration requirements.

Robert Andras was convinced that Canada would only obtain a decent *Immigration Act* when an answer was found to the basic question "Why do we have immigration to this country?" If a consensus could be reached on the role played by immigration in modern industrial Canada, then perhaps, concluded Andras, this country stood a better chance of getting an exemplary new *Immigration Act*.

In his quest to find answers to this fundamental question, the Minister invited the provinces and any interested organizations to submit briefs. He also commissioned a study to provide a factual background to policy issues and furnish policy options. The green paper was intended to provoke discussion, and indeed, after its tabling in the House of Commons in February 1975, it unleashed an unprecedented nation-wide debate on immigration policy. Subsequently, a Special Joint Senate–House of Commons Committee was struck to stage public hearings on the controversial paper. After holding 50 public hearings in 21 cities across Canada and reviewing more than 1,400 briefs submitted to it, the hard-working committee produced a report whose recommendations formed the basis of a new *Immigration Act*.

The Immigration Act, 1976

The *Immigration Act*, the cornerstone of present-day immigration policy, was enacted in 1976 and came into force in 1978. It broke new ground by spelling out the fundamental principles and objectives of Canadian immigration policy. Included among these are the promotion of Canada's demographic, economic, cultural, and social goals; family reunification; the fulfillment of Canada's international obligations in relation to the United Nations Convention (1951) and its 1967 Protocol relating to refugees, which Canada had signed in 1969; non-discrimination in immigration policy; and cooperation between all levels of government and the voluntary sector in the settlement of immigrants in Canadian society.

Among the Act's other important innovations is a provision requiring the government to plan immigration (that is, to set target numbers for different classifications of immigrants, etc.) and to consult with the provinces regarding the planning and management of Canadian immigration. The inclusion of an identifiable class for refugees, selected and admitted separately from immigrants, is another significant innovation in the new Act.

The Act recognizes four basic categories of individuals eligible for landed-immigrant status: (1) family class, which includes the immediate family and dependent children, as well as parents and grandparents over 60, or if widowed or incapable of earning a livelihood, under 60; (2) humanitarian class, which includes (a) refugees as defined in the 1951 United Nations Convention relating to refugees and (b) persecuted and displaced persons who do not qualify as refugees under the rigid UN definition but who are members of a specially designated class created by the Cabinet for humanitarian reasons; (3) independent class, which comprises applicants who apply for landed-immigrant status on their own initiative and are selected on the basis of the points system; and (4) assisted relatives, that is, more distant relatives who are sponsored by a family member in Canada and who meet some of the selection criteria of the independent class.

The 1976 *Immigration Act* received almost unanimous support from all parties in the House as well as the widespread approval of public and private interest groups, the media, and academics. Nearly all these interested observers lauded it as a liberal and progressive measure.

The 1977 Citizenship Act

In the wake of the new *Immigration Act* came the 1977 *Citizenship Act*, whose provisions on nationality are still in force today. This act defines "citizen" as a "Canadian citizen" and declares that not only are naturalized and native-born citizens equally entitled to all the powers, rights, and privileges of a citizen, they are also equally subject to all the obligations, duties, and liabilities of a citizen.

Although the 1947 *Canadian Citizenship Act* had been an immediate success, it was not without flaws. One was the discriminatory treatment of future Canadians. Under the 1947 Act, all non-Canadians, including those who were British subjects (British subjects were defined as citizens of Australia, Ceylon, India, New Zealand, Southern Rhodesia, Republic of South Africa and the United Kingdom), had to wait five years before becoming naturalized. But as modern parlance has it, that is where the level playing field ended when it came to applying for Canadian citizenship. For, unlike an alien (defined by the Act as a "person who is not a Canadian citizen, Commonwealth citizen, British subject, or citizen of the Republic of Ireland"), a British subject could qualify for Canadian citizenship without being called before a judge for a hearing or taking the oath of allegiance in a formal ceremony.

Thanks to changing attitudes and the soaring numbers of non-British immigrants in the 1950s and 1960s, the distinction in treatment between British subjects and aliens began to come under attack. The concept that citizenship is a privilege and not a right was also being questioned. In June 1967, for example, during the course of discussing some amendments to the *Canadian Citizenship Act,* one Member of Parliament observed:

> *Those of us who are natural born citizens are increasingly coming to question whether this concept is one that should be perpetuated forever. We are coming to believe that a legally admitted landed immigrant who has been in this country a reasonable period of time should acquire the right to become a citizen…. I am suggesting that this artificial distinction of a right which exists by virtue of birth in Canada as against birth somewhere else on this small planet is one that should be examined.*

It was to rectify such anomalies and the unequal treatment accorded different groups of people that *An Act Respecting Citizenship* was first introduced in the House of Commons in May 1974. It received Royal Assent on 16 July 1976 and came into force, along with the Citizenship Regulations, on 15 February 1977. Henceforth, improved access and equal treatment of all applicants would be the guiding principles in the granting of Canadian citizenship.

New faces in the immigration queue

The changes set in motion by the abolition of Canada's racist immigration policy and the introduction of the points system did not take long to become apparent. In 1966, 87 percent of Canada's immigrants had been of European origin, while only four years later 50 percent came from quite different regions of the world: the West Indies, Guyana, Haiti, Hong Kong, India, the Philippines, and Indochina. Throughout the 1970s and 1980s, newcomers would more often than not have emigrated from Africa, Asia, the Caribbean, or Latin America; and they would settle in disproportionate numbers in the lower Fraser Valley (the heavily populated area extending from Hope, British Columbia, to Vancouver), the Toronto area, and the greater Montréal region. To even the casual observer, it was obvious that visible ethnic and racial minorities were becoming a significant part of Canada's social fabric. By contrast, other parts of the country, such as the four Atlantic provinces, remained virtually untouched by this immigration.

Refugees

After Canada removed racial and geographical discrimination from its immigration policy and belatedly signed the Geneva Convention relating to the Status of Refugees and its 1967 Protocol (Canada signed in 1969), refugees from outside Europe could apply for and frequently gain admission to this country.

As if to signal the import of these changes, Allan MacEachen, then Minister of Manpower and Immigration, declared in 1969, "Greater attention will be given to the acceptance of refugees for settlement in Canada from other parts of the world."

Fittingly enough, the Minister made this promise the year after Canada began accepting Czechs who had fled their homeland when Warsaw Pact troops crushed an uprising intended to remove Czechoslovakia from the Soviet sphere of influence. Before the end of 1969, Canada would admit approximately 12,000 of these refugees. In the 1970s, the government would have many an opportunity to admit other groups of refugees and, in so doing, live up to its promise. In this decade Ottawa and the Canadian people would find themselves judged by their response to the fallout from the large international refugee movements that attracted so much attention in these years.

Refugees from Tibet

Expressed intentions were translated into action in 1971 and 1972 when Canada admitted some 228 Tibetans. Along with their fellow countrymen, these refugees had fled their homeland after China occupied it in 1959. Led by their Dalai Lama or spiritual leader,

Asian immigrants boarding plane at Entebbe Airport, Uganda, 1972.

Roger St. Vincent Collection

they had sought sanctuary in Nepal, but they were not welcome there. India, however, furnished them with as much assistance as it could. In 1966, the Office of the UN High Commissioner for Refugees tried to interest Canada in accepting some of the Tibetans, all of whom were agriculturalists, for permanent resettlement. Canada turned down the proposal that they be settled on land in groups.

There the matter might have died but for the interest that a later Canadian High Commissioner to India, James George, took in their plight. In the late 1960s, largely through his efforts, plans were devised to bring this small group to Canada,

A group of U.S. Army deserters who fled to Canada and reunited at the American Deserters Committee, Montréal, Quebec, 7 February 1970.

National Archives of Canada (PA 153762)

where, despite initial difficulties, they adapted quickly and successfully to Canadian life.

The Ugandan Asians

Among the newcomers accepted from Africa in these years was a group of well-trained and highly educated Asians who had been expelled from Uganda by Idi Amin's decree of August 1972. In response to an urgent appeal from the British government, Pierre Trudeau's Liberal government decided to accept some 5,000 of these refugees. However, despite the opposition parties' tacit agreement with the decision, the government moved cautiously, sensing marked public opposition to the exercise and fearing a backlash if the Asians were granted special concessions. Only when the situation grew more critical with the approach of the deportation deadline did Ottawa relax the points system and medical requirements for the Asians. Eventually 4,420 of these refugees entered Canada, arriving on an emergency airlift conducted between October and November 1972. Another 1,278 Ugandan Asians followed them in the first half of 1973.

Draft-age Americans in Canada

American draft-dodgers and military deserters who sought refuge in Canada during the Vietnam War would ignite even more controversy, some of it provoked by the Canadian government's initial refusal to admit those who could not prove that they had been discharged from military service (this changed in 1968). Draft-dodgers were usually college-educated sons of the middle class who could no longer defer induction into the Selective Service System; deserters, on the other hand, were predominantly sons of the lower-income and working classes who had been inducted into the armed services directly from high school or who had volunteered, hoping to obtain a skill and broaden their limited horizons.

90

Starting in 1965, Canada became a choice haven for American draft-dodgers and deserters. Because they were not formally classified as refugees but were admitted as immigrants, there is no official estimate of how many draft-dodgers and deserters were admitted to Canada during the Vietnam War. One informed estimate puts their number between 30,000 and 40,000. Whether or not this estimate is accurate, the fact remains that immigration from the United States was high as long as the war raged and that in 1971 and 1972 Canada received more immigrants from the United States than from any other country. Although some of these transplanted Americans returned home after the Vietnam War, most of them put down roots in Canada, making up the largest, best-educated group this country had ever received.

Refugees from Chile

Further controversy was unleashed when over 7,000 Chilean and other Latin American refugees were admitted to Canada after the violent overthrow of Salvador Allende's democratically elected Socialist–Communist government in

Arrival of a small boat with 162 Vietnamese refugees on board. The boat sank a few metres from the shore. Most of the refugees were rescued and reached the coast safely.

UNHCR/K. Gaugler

1973. Chilean and non-Chilean supporters of the old regime had fled the oppression directed against them by Chile's new military ruler, General Pinochet, in the wake of the coup.

Although Canada took the refugees in, it did so grudgingly—at least initially. Despite pressure from Amnesty International, church, labour, and Latino groups, the government was slow to react, not wanting to antagonize Chile's new administration and the United States, which had deplored Chile's slide into economic chaos under Allende. Ideological rather than racial considerations had apparently become a

determining factor in Canada's admissions policy.

The boat people

This country was far more humanitarian in its response to the plight of the "boat people," Vietnamese, Laotians, and Kampucheans who fled Communist regimes in the wake of Saigon's

Michael Ondaatje: Writer and Filmmaker

Anyone who has seen *The English Patient* instinctively recognizes it as one of the most haunting, harrowing, and beautiful films ever made. But does the viewer also realize that it is based on an award-winning novel written by a Canadian, and that this same Canadian co-authored the film's script?

Michael Ondaatje has gained an international reputation as a Canadian novelist, poet, and filmmaker, but he was actually born in Colombo, Ceylon (Sri Lanka), on 12 September 1943, to a privileged and exotic family of Dutch, Sinhalese, and Tamil ancestry. In 1962, he emigrated to Canada via England, where he had studied at Dulwich College, London.

Ondaatje continued his formal education at Bishop's University in Lennoxville, Quebec (1962–64), at University College, University of Toronto, where he obtained a BA in 1965, and at Queen's University, which awarded him a master's degree in 1967.

The author's first collections of poetry include *The Dainty Monsters* (1967), *The Man with Seven Toes* (1969), and *Rat Jelly* (1973). *The Collected Works of Billy the Kid* (poetry and prose), a factual and fictional recreation of the life of the celebrated outlaw, won the Governor General's Award in 1970. It has been adapted for stage and produced at Toronto, New York, and Stratford.

His book *Coming through Slaughter* (1976) employs fiction, fact, and poetry in a recounting of real and imagined events in the life of New Orleans jazz cornetist, Buddy Bolden, while *Running in the Family* (1982) depicts the unconventional lives of Ondaatje's parents and grandparents. A book of collected poems written between 1963 and 1978, *There's a Trick with a Knife I'm Learning to Do*, won him a second Governor General's Award in 1979. *In the Skin of a Lion* (1987), a novel set in Toronto, received the Trillium award.

Michael Ondaatje also has several films to his credit, including *Sons of Captain Poetry*, which is about the poet bp Nichol, *Carry On Crime and Punishment*, *The Clinton Special*, which deals with Theatre Passe Muraille's Farm Show, and *Royal Canadian Hounds*.

The author and filmmaker has combined his writing with teaching at York University, Toronto, and editing collections of poems and stories. He will probably be best-known, however, for his novel, *The English Patient*, which not only garnered a Governor General's Award for fiction (1992) and the coveted Booker Prize but also inspired the film that won nine Academy awards.

fall in 1975. In 1979 and 1980, Canada accepted approximately 60,000 of these refugees, most of whom had endured several days in small, leaky boats, prey to vicious pirate attacks, before ending up in squalid camps in Thailand and Malaysia. Their numbers were such that they comprised 25 percent of all the newcomers to this country between 1978 and 1981, a very high proportion given that refugees normally make up only about 10 percent of the annual flow to Canada.

It was not until 1978, however, that the movement of the boat people to Canada gained momentum. Its springboard was the announcement that Canada would offer a home to 600 refugees on board the *Hai Hong,* which the Malaysian government had refused permission to dock. In the following year, the defeat of the Liberals and their replacement by Joe Clark's Progressive Conservative government coincided with a dramatic increase in the number of refugees fleeing Vietnam. In response to intensive lobbying by church congregations and other organizations in the voluntary sector, the government announced in July 1979 that it would admit 50,000 refugees to Canada by the end of 1980. The decision provided for both privately sponsored and government-sponsored refugees, the government initially agreeing to match each refugee that individuals and church and other voluntary groups supported. Thanks in large part to the Clark government's generous response, some 77,000 Indo-Chinese refugees entered Canada between 1975 and 1981.

Provincial interest in immigration

A provision in the 1976 *Immigration Act* that authorizes the minister to enter into agreements with the provinces to facilitate the drawing up and implementation of immigration policies helped to inspire the negotiation of several federal–provincial immigration agreements in the 1970s. The most far-reaching of these—and the one that attracted the most press coverage—was the agreement concluded in 1978 with Quebec, the Cullen–Couture Agreement.

In the first decades after the Second World War, Quebeckers and their politicians took little interest in the positive role that immigration could play in the economic and cultural development of the province. This attitude began to change during the Quiet Revolution of the 1960s when the Jean Lesage Liberal government announced the creation of a Quebec immigration service in 1965. Essentially an exercise on paper, this initiative was eclipsed in 1968 by the Union Nationale government's establishment of an immigration department to promote the integration of immigrants into Quebec's Francophone society. That same year, the Quebec government signed an agreement with Ottawa to place Quebec officials in federal immigration offices abroad to assist in the selection of suitable immigrants for Quebec. This was followed seven years later by the Entente Bienvenue–Andras, which authorized Quebec to interview prospective immigrants and to make recommendations to federal visa officers.

When the Parti Québécois came to power under René Lévesque in 1976, it assigned top billing to immigration. In fact, immigration was one of the first issues that the new government raised with Ottawa, with Quebec pushing for a full range of powers in this field. Two years later the Cullen–Couture Agreement was concluded. This milestone agreement declared that immigration to Quebec must contribute to the province's cultural and social development and provided the province with a say in the selection of independent-class immigrants (skilled workers and businessmen with their dependents) and refugees abroad. In addition, the agreement allowed the province to determine financial and other criteria for family-class and assisted-relative sponsorship.

Multiculturalism

Multiculturalism was another immigration-related issue that surfaced during the 1970s. The concept was thrust into the political limelight on 8 October 1971, when Pierre Trudeau announced in the House of Commons that his government would adopt a policy of multiculturalism within a bilingual framework.

When he made this warmly received announcement, Trudeau failed to explain why his government was officially adopting such a concept. He carefully refrained from mentioning that multiculturalism was intended to persuade non-English and non-French Canadians to accept official bilingualism, the federal policy that had been instituted in 1969 with the passage of the *Official Languages Act*. Designed to promote the equality of French and English in all federal government operations, official bilingualism had been urged by the Royal Commission on Bilingualism and Biculturalism (the B&B Commission), which had been established in 1963 to inquire into the use of French and the status of French Canadians in Canada. To its sponsors, the policy of bilingualism seemed to be a logical response to the tumultuous nationalism that shook Quebec in the 1960s. Nevertheless, it never received widespread support.

From its inception, official bilingualism stirred up opposition across the country. Nowhere, however, did it attract more hostility than in the West. Westerners of Ukrainian, German, or other non-English or non-French backgrounds demanded to know why the federal government assigned less importance to their culture than to that of the

Wilder Penfield:
Medical Pioneer and Author

The neurosurgeon and scientist Wilder Penfield (1891–1976) certainly stands out among the American immigrants who have made outstanding contributions to Canada. Dr. Penfield's remarkable achievements in medicine won him high praise both in Canada and abroad and brought increased recognition to the Montréal medical community.

Born in Spokane, Washington, in 1891, Wilder Penfield obtained a BLitt from Princeton University in 1913. He then attended Merton College, Oxford, where he was influenced by two great medical teachers, the celebrated Canadian physician Sir William Osler, who became his lifelong hero, and the prominent neurophysiologist Charles Sherrington. After obtaining an MD from Johns Hopkins University in 1918, the young doctor served as surgeon at the Presbyterian Hospital (affiliated with Columbia University) in New York and at the New York Neurological Institute, 1921–28.

In 1928, Penfield became professor of neurology and neurosurgery at McGill University in Montréal. There, pursuing the puzzle of epilepsy, he undertook a systematic mapping of the human brain and, with associates, produced scientific papers, handbooks, and monographs that became standard reference works on the function of the brain.

When the Montréal Neurological Institute opened in 1934, Wilder

Penfield became the inaugural director of the first institution in the world to be devoted exclusively to the treatment of nerve disease. Its formal opening on 27 September of that year climaxed several years of planning in which the surgeon and teacher had played a leading role. In his new capacity, Dr. Penfield presided over an institute whose task, as he so aptly defined it, was "the achievement of a greater understanding of the ills to which the nervous system is heir, to the end that we may come to the bedside with healing in our hands."

Although Wilder Penfield retired in 1960, he continued to lead a very active life, becoming the first director of the Vanier Institute of the Family, a supporter of university education, and the author of several books. His writings from the last 15 years of his life include *The Mystery of the Mind* (1975), which summarizes his views on the mind–brain problem; and *No Man Alone* (1977), an autobiography of his early years, 1891–1934. Earlier works include two historical novels—*No Other Gods* (1954) and *The Torch* (1960)—which found a wide readership.

Wilder Penfield's most lasting legacy is undoubtedly his work with the internationally renowned Montréal Neurological Institute. The hospital, which has been integrated with a brain-research complex, is recognized to this day as a centre for the study of the human brain. It also serves as a model for similar units around the world.

much smaller French-speaking minorities in Western Canada.

The Trudeau government responded to the increasing assertiveness of the so-called "third force" in Canadian society by adopting recommendations made by the B&B Commission that would safeguard the contributions of other "ethnic" groups (excluding the Native peoples) to Canada's cultural enrichment. These recommendations called for a policy of multiculturalism within a bilingual framework. Multiculturalism itself was not new. It was merely an old activity given a new name. But no matter what its guise, those who espoused it sought to promote equality and respect among Canada's different ethnic or cultural groups.

To implement its new policy, the government appointed a Minister Responsible for Multiculturalism in 1972 and in 1973 set up a Canadian Multiculturalism Council and the Multiculturalism Directorate within the Department of the Secretary of State. Like official bilingualism, however, multiculturalism would invite opposition, much of which would develop during the turbulent eighties, when

Canada faced some of the most challenging immigration issues ever to confront policy-makers and try the souls of policy-enforcers.

What does the future hold?

The immigration patterns that have figured so prominently in altering the face of present-day Canada's largest cities were well under way when Trudeau announced his government's multiculturalism policy in 1971. Just as these patterns were the direct result of the government's decision in the 1960s to reject Canada's racist immigration policy, so too was the rapid colonization and development of the Prairie provinces a direct consequence of the government's decision to promote the immigration of "stalwart peasants in sheepskin coats." It is progressive decisions like these that have opened the country's doors to successive waves of immigrants, each with a contribution to make. These timely political decisions have helped to create the vibrant Canada that we know today, a Canada whose growing confidence was expressed in the *Canadian Citizenship Act* of 1947 and its successor, the

Citizenship Act of 1977. What decisions, one must wonder, will govern immigration policy in the years ahead and how will the resulting immigration shape the Canada of the future?

Sources

[Abella, Rosalie]. "Welcome to Pier 21. Welcome to Canada." *The Globe and Mail* [Toronto], 2 July 1999.

Avery, Donald. *'Dangerous Foreigners': European Immigrant Workers and Labour Radicalism in Canada, 1896–1932.* Toronto: McClelland and Stewart, 1979.

Bata, Thomas. *Shoemaker to the World.* Toronto: Stoddart, 1990.

Brown, Robert Craig and Ramsay Cook. *Canada 1896–1921: A Nation Transformed.* Toronto: McClelland and Stewart, 1974.

Canada. Citizenship and Immigration Canada. Unpublished statistics.

Colombo, John Robert. *Colombo's Canadian References.* Toronto: Oxford University Press, 1976.

Corpus Information Services et al. *The Canadian Family Tree.* Toronto and Ottawa: Corpus Information Services with the Multiculturalism Directorate, Department of the Secretary of State and the Canadian Government Publishing Centre, Supply and Services Canada, 1979.

Creighton, Donald. *The Forked Road: Canada 1939–1957.* Toronto: McClelland and Stewart, 1976.

Department of Canadian Heritage. Historic Sites and Monuments Board of Canada. Background file on Cyril Genik.

Gwyn, Sandra. *Tapestry of War: A Private View of Canadians in the Great War.* Toronto: HarperCollins, 1992.

Hamilton, Robert and Dorothy Shields. *The Dictionary of Canadian Quotations and Phrases.* Rev. ed. Toronto: McClelland and Stewart, 1979.

Hawkins, Freda. *Critical Years in Immigration: Canada and Australia Compared.* Kingston and Montréal: McGill-Queen's University Press, 1989.

Ignatieff, George. *The Making of a Peacemonger: The Memoirs of George Ignatieff.* Toronto: University of Toronto Press, 1985.

Ivany, Kathryn. "A Colony of Britons." Horizon Canada 7, 82: 1958–63.

Keenleyside, Hugh. *Memoirs of Hugh L. Keenleyside.* Vol. 2. Toronto: McClelland and Stewart, 1982.

Kelly, Ninette and Michael Trebilcock. *The Making of a Mosaic: A History of Canadian Immigration Policy.* Toronto: University of Toronto Press, 1998.

Knowles, Valerie. *Strangers at Our Gates: Canadian Immigration and Immigration Policy, 1540–1997.* Rev. ed. Toronto: Dundurn, 1997.

Krawchuk, Peter, ed. *Reminiscences of Courage and Hope: Stories of Ukrainian Women Pioneers.* Trans. Michael Ukas. Toronto: Kobzar, 1991.

Lehr, John. "Land's Sake." Horizon Canada 3, 36: 854–59.

Marchildon, Gregory. *Profits and Politics: Beaverbrook and the Gilded Age of Canadian Finance.* Toronto: University of Toronto Press, 1996.

Martin, Paul. Far From Home. Vol. 1 of *A Very Public Life*. Ottawa: Deneau, 1984.

McInnes, Marvin. "Migration." Plate 27. In Addressing the Twentieth Century, 1891–1961, edited by Donald Kerr, Deryck W. Holdsworth and Susan L. Laskin. Vol. 3 of *Historical Atlas of Canada*. Toronto: University of Toronto Press, 1990.

Morton, Desmond. *A Short History of Canada*. Edmonton: Hurtig, 1983.

Multiculturalism and Citizenship Canada. *The Evolution of Citizenship Legislation in Canada*, by William Kaplan. Ottawa: Multiculturalism and Citizenship Canada, 1991.

National Archives of Canada. Robert Borden Papers. MG26H, vol. 336.

Organization for Economic Co-operation and Development. *Trends in International Migration: Annual Report, 1998*. Paris: OECD, 1998.

Parliament. House of Commons. Debates. April 1902; July 1903; May 1906; June 1906; October 1945; May 1947; June 1973; July 1973.

"'Policy' at Bankrupt Level." Editorial. *The Globe and Mail* [Toronto], 28 May 1947.

Potestio, John. "From Navvies to Contractors: The History of Vincenzo and Giovanni Veltri, Founders of R.F. Welch Ltd., 1885–1931." M.A. thesis, Lakehead University, 1981.

Potvin, Rose, ed. *Passion and Conviction: The Letters of Graham Spry*. Regina: Plains Research Centre, University of Regina, 1992.

Ramirez, Bruno. "Italian Roots," Horizon Canada 1, 7: 164–68.

Statistics Canada. *Canada 1950: The Official Handbook of Present Conditions and Recent Progress*. Ottawa: Dominion Bureau of Statistics, 1950. Statistics Canada. World Wide Web site: http://www.statcan.ca

Story, Norah. *The Oxford Companion to Canadian History and Literature*. Toronto: Oxford University Press, 1967.

Sunahara, Ann. "Japanese." In *The Canadian Encyclopedia*, 2: 1104–5. 2nd ed. Edmonton: Hurtig, 1988.

Urquhart, M.C., ed. *Historical Statistics of Canada*. Toronto: Macmillan, 1965.

Veltri, Giovanni. *Memoirs of Giovanni Veltri*. Trans. John Potestio. Toronto: Multicultural History Society and Ontario Heritage Foundation, 1987.

Whetton, Cecilia. *The Promised Land: The Story of the Barr Colonists*. Lloydminster: Lloydminster Times [1953].

Index

Freiman, Lillian, 54

Genik, Cyril, 29

George, James, 89

German, W.M., 33

Grands Ballets Canadiens, 77

Green, George Everitt, 22

Green Paper of 1974, 85, 86

guest children from Great Britain. See immigration, guest children

Hai Hong (ship), 92

Harris, Walter, 73

home children. See immigration, home children

Howe, C.D., 71

Hutterites, See immigration, Hutterite

Ignatieff, George, 49

immigration: African, 88; agriculturalists during Sifton regime, 9-14, 17, 18, 22-25; during Oliver years, 35, 40; American, 2, 9-11, 40, 52, 90, 91; Asian, 2, 25, 26, 36, 88; Balts, 69, 70, 77; blacks, 10, 11; border inspection service, 39; British, 2, 3, 18-25, 35, 36, 44, 53, 66; Caribbean, 88; Central American, 88; Chinese, 2, 37, demographic role of, 4; departments, 83; Doukhobor, 17, 18, 52, 53; Dutch, 70; "enemy aliens," 46, 48, 50-52; family class, 87; First World War, 46; German, 13, 14, 52, 72; during Great Depression of the 1930s, 55; guest children from Great Britain, 60; home children, 19-22; Hutterite, 52; impact on economy, 4; on population, 1, 2; independent class, 87, 93; Indian, 26; Italian, 14-17, 72; Japanese, 25, 26; Jewish, 47, 54; Mennonite, 14, 52, 53; Norwegian, 26, 27; opposition to, 27, 28, 36, 50, 55, 56; Polish, 67; post-war boom (1947-57), 66-76; pro-immigration lobby (1946-52), 58, 59; repatriation of French Canadians, 14; riots over (See Vancouver Riot of 1907); Russian, 17, 18, 49; Salvation Army's role in, 19; Scandinavian, 26; Sikh, 26; South American, 88; Ukrainian, 5, 11-13, 29, 40

Immigration Act: of 1906, 32, 33; revisions, 38; of 1910, 33, 34; revisions, 51, 52; of 1952, 72, 73, 79, 85, 86; of 1976, 86, 87

Immigration Appeal Board, 84, 85

immigration promotion, 9, 53

immigration regulations: 1962, 81, 82

Japanese Canadians. See discrimination, Japanese Canadians as victims during the Second World War

Keenleyside, Hugh, 69

King, Mackenzie, 36, 38, 66; and Asian immigration, 38; immigration policy statement, 1947, 67, 68

Kizyma, Senefta, 5

Komagata Maru (ship), 38, 39

Laurier, Sir Wilfrid, 7, 43

League of Nations Society in Canada, 59

Lévesque, René, 93

Lloyd, Rev. George, 22-24

Macdonald, Sir John A., 7, 9

MacEachen, Allan, 88, 89

Macpherson, Annie, 20

Mennonites. See immigration, Mennonite

Monk, Frederick, 33

multiculturalism, 93-95

North Atlantic Trading Company, 12, 34, 35

Oliver, Frank, 28, 31, 32, 35, 36, 39

Ondaatje, Michael, 92

Papineau, Talbot, 45

Pearson, Lester B., 45